ANANDA YOGA

CONVERSATIONS ON HAPPINESS

" Real Masters don't die and those who die are not Real Masters. Real Masters guide their own (who are totally surrendered unto them) with their divine magic even after centuries have gone by. "

SWAMI SHRI HARISH MADHUKAR

ANANDA YOGA

CONVERSATIONS ON HAPPINESS

with
Swami Shri Harish Madhukar
(Babaji)

BY MANDAKINI TRIVEDI

A Division of Maoli Media Private Limited

Ananda Yoga: Conversations on Happiness with Swami Shri Harish Madhukar (Babaji)

Earlier published by Tripura Publications
First Edition 2005
Second Edition 2006

First Zen Publications Edition March 2019

PUBLISHED BY
ZEN PUBLICATIONS
A Division of Maoli Media Private Limited
60, Juhu Supreme Shopping Centre,
Gulmohar Cross Road No. 9, JVPD Scheme,
Juhu, Mumbai 400 049. India.
Tel: +91 9022208074
eMail: info@zenpublications.com
Website: www.zenpublications.com

IN COLLABORATION WITH

SHAKTIYOGASHRAMA GURUKULAM
Telbaila, Taluka Mulshi, District Pune, Maharashtra 412108. India.
Regd. Public Trust (Regd. No. E-2052. Pune Division Dated 02.09.95

eMail: shaktiyogashrama@gmail.com
Website: www.shaktiyogashrama.com

ISBN 978-93-87242-41-8

अज्ञानतिमिरान्धस्य ज्ञानाञ्जनशलाकया
चक्षुरुन्मिलितं येन तस्मै श्रीगुरवे नमः।

The darkness of Ignorance
He who has removed, by opening my eyes,
And adorning them
With the kohl of Knowledge,
To that Satguru I bow.

DEDICATED AT THE FEET OF

SWAMI SHRI HARISH MADHUKAR (Babaji),

THE LIGHT OF MY LIFE,

THE CENTRE OF MY CONSCIOUSNESS.

Mandakini Trivedi with Babaji

About The Author

Mandakini Trivedi is the lineage bearer of Swami Shri Harish Madhukar's sampradaya. Swamiji initiated her into many spiritual practices of the Sri Vidya path, as she lived and learnt from him. But it was his philosophy of Ananda Yoga or Integrated Happiness, which merged spirituality seamlessly with life - that had the greatest influence on her life and art.

The teaching method of Swamiji, or Babaji as he was lovingly known, could neither be called a 'method', nor could it be called 'teaching'. He lived the teaching and the disciple learnt through direct experience & perception. Mandakini had the good fortune of spending a lot of time with The Master - travelling with him, reading with him, spending time at the ashram with him, watching his interactions with ordinary people, observing him go about routine chores in the most extraordinary ways, both cheerfully & mindfully. Each of these was a powerful learning experience that groomed her.

A dancer by profession, Mandakini found her true understanding of classical Indian Dance only after meeting Babaji. He seemed to embody all that was described in texts on Indian aesthetics, as the essence & purpose of the arts - JOY!

Spirituality & Art have come a full circle, becoming one with her persona. It is only due to the grace of Babaji, that Mandakini has been able to do pioneering work in the field of The Yoga of Indian Dance. She passes on this understanding to the next generation at the Nateshvari Dance Gurukul.

She has also authored 'The Yoga Of Indian Dance' & 'Sutras On Dance' to express her insights on the element of sadhana, in classical Indian Dance. In 2016, she was awarded the Sangeet Natak Akademi Award for her work in Mohini Attam.

Before Babahi shed his mortal form, he founded the Shaktiygashrama Gurukul, appointing Mandakini as its chairperson. Under Mandakini's guidance, the ashram conducts residential programmes that integrate Spirituality, Ecology, Art, Wellness & Holistic Lifestyles to express the common thread of Yoga that runs through them. The ashram is also involved in rural, educational programmes.

Mandakini's life is devoted to fulfilling her gurus work & vision in the field of spirituality, art and education.

MY SINCEREST THANKS TO

Sketches : Tripurari Singh

Cover page and book-design : Miti Desai

Cover Photograph : Shivani Gupta

Calligraphy : R.K Joshi, Achyut Palav

Proofreading & continuous support :
Gauri Kshirsagar, Kanhaiya Solegaonkar and Snehal Solegaonkar

Suggestions on the primary manuscripts :
Bharati Nirmal and Jinendra Kothari

Editing : Nisha Ravi, Suryakant Trivedi, Anjali Bhelande

All *'sevaks'* and donors, past and present, for supporting the ashram by giving their time and energy.

- Mandakini Trivedi

Compiled from reminiscences by :

Mukunda Mane, Snehal Solegaonkar, Kanhaiya Solegaonkar,
Gauri Kshirsagar, Jinendra Kothari, Datta Urne,
Maganbhai Raj Purohit, Ramesh Vyas,
Suryakant Trivedi and Mandakini Trivedi.

Contents

Foreword

My little nephew was once asked -

"What does this Babaji, who comes to your house, do?"

"Oh nothing", he quipped, "he simply sits and talks the whole day"

These very 'talks' have shifted perceptions and shaped the lives of disciples. These simple exchanges have provided vital clues to spiritual *sadhana*. And these seemingly homely conversations have broken down the barriers between life and *sadhana*.

Disciples are often asked, "What was Babaji's method of teaching?" I think if there is any one single method that he used consistently and universally, with young and old, rich and poor, disciples and non-disciples, it was that of simple sharing through conversations, chatting, joking, commenting on practical problems and situations and turning them inside out, to reveal a whole new side to life. In a way, through these conversations, he taught us how to operate from another level of Consciousness while dealing with mundane life.

For me and for many others, the greatest learning has happened through simple conversations that we had with him, while doing the ordinary chores of life like chopping vegetables, cleaning the room, cooking, traveling by bus or train or simply discussing the day's events.

People who came to him with a view to be instantly enlightened, or with the purpose of 'decorating' themselves with more knowledge, often went back disappointed, doubting whether he had any experience of Truth at all.

Babaji had the knack of turning all timetables and programmes topsy-turvy! He could indefinitely delay a *puja*, if a situation or event allowed him to have a dialogue on life and the finer points of Truth. This honing of awareness he would say is the real *puja* -'*chaitanyarghya samaradhya, chaitanya kusumapriya* - offer god the oblations and flower of awareness and purity.' Needless to say, ritualists went back disgruntled and disgusted. "Why", he would often ask, "is the world so obsessed with doing and painful effort, why does life have meaning for people only if they exert themselves? Why, if they come to the *ashram*, they want to engage in severe penance and 'doing' *dhyana* or meditation! This is all donkeywork - even if it may be 'spiritual'!"

I did not even realize that there can be other ways of learning, till after he passed away and I was made aware of the plethora of meditation courses – for beginners, intermediate and advanced levels – that were a part of any *ashram's* activities. People started asking me what were the techniques that were taught at *Shaktiyogashrama* and what were the courses that were to be conducted to propagate his teachings. I was dumb struck - how can one make techniques out of conversational exchanges that seamlessly merged life with spiritual *sadhana*?

My very first interaction with Babaji at the *ashram*, set the pace for his simple method of teaching, while shattering my concept of learning.

It was 12 noon. I had come to learn meditation from him because I believed that is what one had to do to evolve, and I was in a hurry to evolve! I had just a couple of hours before the last bus came in. And that was the only time I could spare, to carry some peace of mind or techniques to achieve that, before I came back to the city.

On reaching the *ashram*, I hurriedly put down my bags, while he got busy in making me comfortable, arranging for the refreshments etc. I felt I must make my intentions very clear before any more time was wasted in these trivial formalities, so I blurted out – "Babaji I have come to learn *dhyana*." He looked at me mischievously and said, "For that you will have to spend the night here." "Oh, that's impossible" I said, "I have to catch the next bus." "In that case," he said, "let's enjoy a good meal together". And so saying, he got busy in preparing the food. The bus did not arrive on schedule - it was delayed by more than an hour. As I waited at the bus-stop with Babaji, my irritation and anxiety increased. I was restless at the possibilities and consequences of this inordinate delay in the travel plans. Sensing this Babaji suddenly quipped, "Let me teach you how to meditate!" "What!" I said, "now? Now my mind is restless and unable to focus." "Precisely," he said, "that's when you have to sit and meditate!"

The bus eventually did arrive and yes, my spiritual journey did begin.

This book is a compilation of Babaji's simple dialogues with disciples, which arose from day to day events. Often the events were so simple and ordinary, and the teaching even simpler, that we missed the point completely and carelessly nodded. Years later however, when we were 'ready', these simple poignant dialogues burst forth with a ring of satori and awakening.

I hope, that somewhere in the heart of the reader, a similar awakening will happen, as he too chats along with Babaji.

While sharing the Truth, Babaji would always say, "This is a debt that I owe to the *gurus*. What I have learnt from them, I have to pass on, or I will have to be reborn to fulfill that debt." Having compiled this garland of conversations, it seems like this (compilation) is also a debt we owe him. The entire exercise has made disciples delve deep into their memory for incidents and interactions that even they had forgotten existed. It has resulted in a *manana* - meditation - on the *guru charitra.*

Above all, simply gathering the brief interactions has made us aware of the large body of guidance that he has left behind. That seemingly small and fragmented treasure, has acquired volume and substance through this collective effort. The compilation is a record of the gist of his teachings and brings to light his syncretic approach to spirituality.

For me personally, this compilation has in a sense, been the fulfillment of a prophecy. Many years back, after we had returned from the Himalayas, he had said, "You have been told by *Gurumaharaj* to write the teachings of the *gurus.*"

I understood it then as, putting on paper my insights on *sadhana,* and the higher truth as it occured to me on my spiritual journey. It was only when this 'book-idea' came to my mind that I realized what Babaji could have meant then. For practical purposes, the authorship of the book has been credited to me; although in actuality I am only an instrument of the *gurumandala.* When they, the *gurus,* have written the story of my life, what credit can I take for a single chapter from that life?

I would also like to pay my respects to Shri Sharad Phatak, my present *yoga* master, learning under whom, has brought me closer to the teachings of Babaji. To me he is the messenger of Babaji, the silent inspiration behind this book.

The work itself has only given joy although not without a sense of responsibility - the responsibility of doing justice to the teachings of Babaji.

Words have a rigid, linear, static and almost stale quality. They cannot fully capture the freshness and dynamism of the living force that the transmission between the teacher and the taught is. Words are passive and open to subjective interpretation. They cannot play the role of a dispassionate master who diagnoses each one's personal problems and prescribes accordingly. Words can be conveniently twisted to suit one's egotistical needs.

However, a master sees through the game of your trickster mind and ego and there is no escaping the bitter pill. As Babaji said, "Words cannot satiate. It is only an experience of the meanings of words that can satiate".In order to get this sense of fulfilment, I would request the reader to make the effort of going through the whole book, for although each conversation may seem complete, reading through the entire book alone can give a sense of the completeness of Babaji's teachings. I would also request the reader to 'rightly understand' the teachings in the light of what a 'Babaji' is.

Yet, if the book does not convey the essence, then the blame lies with the inadequacy of my powers of comprehension and expression, and not in the incompleteness of his teachings. Of course, no words can express the bubbling joy that he brought into my life, nor the beauty of a love that was so fulfilling, that it freed me, once and for all, from the 'need' to be loved. I am sure all disciples have felt this in a greater or lesser measure. It seems like we just gave him enough time to clear the field of weeds and shrubs and sow the seed. Now we have to make that seed grow. This book is a reminder of that.

I would like to thank the disciples and followers of Babaji for entrusting me with their confidence and personal notes. I must confess that some kind of recasting and recreation has gone into the notes and inputs of the disciples, so that the reader gets an idea of the essence of the teachings of Babaji and the mystique of his persona. I hope the disciples and Babaji himself will forgive me for any errors thereof. Names of disciples have deliberately not been mentioned because the guru is One, all *shishyas* are One and the Truth that unites them is One.

The book also contains a monogram on the life sketch of Babaji. This too was revealed through conversations and seems like a legitimate part of the book. The plans and projects of *Shaktiyogashrama gurukulam* as conceived by Babaji and as it stands today.

For practical purposes, the conversations have been broadly grouped into three categories. The first group consists of conversations on Life, the second on spiritual *sadhana* and the third on *gurus*. It is evident that they are not watertight compartments for *gurus* can only talk of Truth.

When visitors confided in Babaji, I would often jokingly ask him as to how long his 'counselling' sessions would last. He would laugh heartily at the use of this modern terminology, for a function that *gurus* through the ages have been successfully fulfilling. The conversations in the first category belong to this type, wherein a life situation is only a take off point but the message is always spiritual. These conversations have a universal appeal and are for both seekers and non-seekers. The second category 'on spiritual *sadhana*' is for 'seekers.' The last category 'on *gurus*' consists of dialogues that reveal the grandeur, mystique and the sheer humanness of the great masters.

The presence of a master automatically provides continuity to the teachings, however random and disjointed they may seem. In his absence, the thematic classification of the conversations is a means of providing continuity and clarity to his teachings on various topics. This however was not Babaji's style of teaching. He defied all structure, spontaneously responding to the situation at hand. In fact, disciples learnt that to pin down Babaji to a structured sharing, was a sure way of inhibiting him.

The choice of the first and last conversation again is deliberate and significant for it is literally and allegorically, the first and last thing, that he had to say about spiritual life. They sum up his approach to spirituality. Few conversations discuss techniques of spiritual practices because, firstly, techniques are subjective prescriptions and are effective only if they are from the mouth of the *guru (gurumukha vidya)*, and secondly, the chief thrust of his teachings was not on the practice of rituals and techniques, but on 'deconditioning' the mind, on 'emptying' oneself and on practising Self Awareness.

Though Babaji wrote many books; in the last few years of his life he had stopped writing. He would say, "You are my books now, let me write in your hearts." This book is a record of all those teachings that he entrusted us with.

Finally, this book is homage to that simple master who communicated so effortlessly and without any fuss. After Babaji passed away, I was surprised to find that expensive courses were 'available' for insights and *sadhanas* that he had casually communicated to us over a cup of tea! I often wonder - did we in our ignorance / arrogance take the Truth for granted because it was so easily revealed?

Dear Master, this little offering is to beg your pardon for our heedlessness then. This offering is also a token of deep gratitude for allowing the great Himalayan tradition of Truth to pass through us. Today in our darkest hours and moments of doubt, these conversations spring up with clarity and lead us on.

"srigurudevacharanarpanamastu"

– Mandakini Trivedi

On Babaji

Known to his disciples as 'Babaji', Swami Shri Harish Madhukar, had no cult following, did not offer any advanced or beginners courses in meditation, nor did he formally teach any *shastras* or philosophy. He communicated the Truth through his life. Visitors from all walks of life and from all parts of the country came to him seeking answers, but in his presence their questions dissolved and they experienced Love. His expressions in words were direct and simple, "I am not this person; and if you see truth in me I will be of use to you. I am only a tap to the great wisdom and vision of the Gurus. If you turn the tap on, the Truth flows, at other times there is nothing to me."

A BRIEF LIFE - SKETCH

Born in Jadla, Nava Shaher district, Punjab, on 27th August 1923, in a family of five brothers and two sisters, Shri Madhukar revealed spiritual inclination at a very early age and could recite the *Bhagavad Gita* at the age of 4.

An interesting story from his childhood was to fortell his later destiny. When Babaji was about 5 years old, some *sadhus* happened to pass through the village. One of them affectionately tried to catch hold of him, while he was playing with his friends, but Babaji ran away. The *sadhu* turned to Babaji's father and said, "How long will he run away from his destiny. He belongs to us and will eventually return to us!"

He did his Post Graduation in Hindi and English from the Lucknow University. Later he burnt his degree, vowing to never take up a job where they needed proof of his education. He married, had six children and in the years that followed, contributed as an art critic, ran a printing press, an advertising agency, and a leather goods manufacturing firm. He enjoyed life to the brim, full of material comforts and sense pleasures.

Then one day a strange sense of renunciation crept over him, a feeling that he had to go beyond this 'frog in the well' existence. He used to lock himself up in a hotel room for days together poring over the scriptures, inventing and practicing different *sadhanas* by himself, coming out of his hibernation only when the needs of the family had to be met. One day, even this sense of duty fell off and overnight he sold off his leather goods factory, distributed the money among his workers and left for the Himalayas. "Surely," he felt, "this philosophy of the *Vedas, Tantras* and *Upanishads* must live in some person. I must find such a *guru*."

The Search

For the next three years he roamed the Himalayas, often surviving only on banana peels; shelter less, penniless, and clueless as to the identity of the Master. Once, as he was lying broken and disheartened, he had a glimpse of a Master whose touch revived him from his fatigue but instead of holding on to the Master, he rushed to the river to quench his thirst. In a flash, the master had disappeared, but he knew now, who his Master was. He was no more clueless. However, as destiny would have it, for another three years he relentlessly searched for the Master he had glimpsed on that fateful day.

His Master

Many were the *gurus* he met during this search, some pretenders, others genuine. But none of them was the face he was looking for. Finally, in the deep recesses of Tunganatha, in the Himalayas, he met his Master Shri Svarupanandaji Saraswati Maharaj. The Master was a silent teacher, who never ate and never moved from his *asana* (sitting position).

His Sadhana (Spiritual Practices)

His Master simply assigned him the task of grazing cows in the Himalayas. Every morning he left home with the cows only to return in the evenings, tired and hungry, surviving on a frugal meal of milk and chickpeas. Grazing cows in the hilly, jagged terrain was tough and took away all his energy, as care had to be taken that the cattle did not fall off the hills or go astray.

Where was the time for real' *sadhana*? For a man of intellect, in search of Truth, the situation was incomprehensible. Surely, truth cannot be found in this menial, mindless act of grazing cows! His ego protested violently. Many a time, in exasperation, he planned to run away; but always returned to surrender.

Over two years had passed after meeting the Master, with what seemed like no spiritual *sadhana* or guidance, until one fine day, he dropped all effort at grazing the cows and sat doing nothing. In the evening, the cows quietly followed him and looked after themselves as he returned to the *ashram*. A great lesson, which was later to become the foundation of his teaching, was learnt – 'We do nothing, Nature alone does.'

The next day, he was summoned by the Master and instructed to live in a cave and do his *'ekanta sadhana'*; this being the meditation done in seclusion.

Six months later, he emerged from the cave. As he touched his Master's feet, he had the divine vision. Now he was given formal *sanyasa-diksha* and renamed Suprabuddhananda Saraswati. In the true tradition of the *siddhas,* the spiritual journey of Swami Harish Madhukar had begun.

His Ashram

On his return from the Himalayas, he lived and moved in the jungles of Sahyadri at Peth Shapur, about 150 km from Mumbai. Here, a small *ashram* was built and for the next 10 years, he guided disciples as they came. In 1992, his *Gurumaharaj* Swami Shri Svarupanandji Saraswati took *mahasamadhi,* passing on the responsibility of the *guru-mandala* on to him. Thereafter, he started initiating disciples and giving *shaktipat diksha* or *mantra diksha* in the tradition of *sri vidya* worship.

In 1995, was laid the foundation of *Shaktiyogashrama Gurukulam,* on a scenic plot of 30 acres of land at village Telbaila, near Lonavla, about 150 kms from Mumbai. It was envisioned as a multi-dimensional educational complex in the form of a mini university, consisting of *Gurukulams* (residential schools) of the classical Indian arts of *nritya* (dance), *sangeet* (music), *chitra* (painting), *vastu/shilpa* (architecture/sculpture); and the classical Indian sciences of *yoga, ayurveda* (medicine) and *jyotish shastra* (astrology). The *ashram-gurukul* was meant to revive the values of holistic living, cultural rootedness and the need for spiritual orientation in education.

It was Swami Shri Harish Madhukar's response to the deteriorating state of education in India. Pained by the pathetic state it (education) was in, he decided to found a *gurukulam* to give people the best in traditional and modern education.

Towards the fulfillment of this dream, he worked like a man possessed. For a year, he worked feverishly, collecting funds, building, promoting and spelling out the vision of the *ashram-gurukul.* On 20th March 1996, on the auspicious day of *Gudi Padva* he inaugurated the *gurukulam* and started holding residential camps therein. On 26th October 1996, he presented the first *Sharadotsava* at the *ashram.*

On 31 October 1996, Swami Harish Madhukar cast off his physical body and merged with the eternal.

His Teachings

His teachings consisted of simple statements made as you sat, ate, chatted, joked, chopped vegetables, strolled, watered the plants or as you tidied his room. He constantly reminded his disciples - 'Realization of truth demands no apparent qualifications. It may happen to anyone, anywhere, anytime, in any manner.

He embraced both external and internal worship or the worship of the form and the formless. Consciousness, he stressed, exists both without and within. Thus, the *sadhanas* he recommended included *pranavabhyasa* or recitation of the *aumkara mantra,* meditation on the Self, *mantra japa* and recitation of *stotras* to harmonise and raise the *kundalini shakti* within. Above all, he advocated a 24-hour *sadhana* of living joyously, in full awareness, free of all conditioning, preferences and prejudices and preconceived notions, under the grace of *Bhagavati Tripura.*

The uniqueness of Babaji's style of teaching was that while most teachings focus on the means and methods, Babaji made the end itself the means. He felt - 'Why not start living right now in That State in which you will eventually live after you have attained. Let the goal become the path, this very moment. There is nowhere to reach. Why waste time in future imaginings. Live the Truth here and now. That is the ultimate *sadhana*.'

He expressed this philosophy in simple assertions that he repeatedly asked his disciples to live by. They were –

- Always be in a state of good cheer - that is the highest *sadhana*.
- Whatever is, is for the best.
- Whatever is, is due to Her Will. Enjoy it, accept it.
- We 'do' nothing. *Bhagvati* 'does'.
- Renounce preferences and prejudices.
- Practice awareness. Be aware of all things at all times.
- You are the awareness of that Awareness.

Conversations with Babaji

सदा
आनंद में
रहना
सबसे
बड़ी
साधना
है

स्वामी हरीश मधुकर

To be in a state of joy, always, is the highest spiritual *sadhana*
– Swami Shri Harish Madhukar

The Highest Sadhana

Babaji was travelling with a disciple by taxi, sharing a few moments before he left for his annual visit to the Himalayas. The disciple was dejected but, as is the case with all those who are new to the path, wanted to put aside her psychological problems and address her spiritual needs.

Babaji : So how are you?

Disciple (in a disheartened tone): Well, OK, but when will you prescribe some sadhana for me? Please give me some sadhana.

Babaji : My dear, to walk through life in utmost good cheer is the highest sadhana, the greatest spiritual discipline.

On Life...

One little agony, one little ecstasy,
One little longing,
One thirst for belonging,
What a pity!
This little piece of eternity,
In search of a destiny.

1. PURPOSE OF LIFE

D[1]: Babaji, what is the purpose of life?
Babaji: To find God. To realise your own Self.
He who has forgotten this chief goal of life has lived in vain.

2. THE BEAR HUG OF SAMSARA

D: But Babaji, this *samsara* does not leave us, much as we try to leave it.
Babaji (laughing): That reminds me of a funny story.
A man was drowning and held on to a piece of blanket floating in the water. A *sadhu* standing on the banks of the river advised him to let go of the blanket, if he wanted to save himself.
The blanket, however, happened to be the fur of a bear that was in the water that had gripped the man. Therefore, the man shouted back "I have left the blanket, but it is not leaving me!"
This *samsara* is like that. If you are caught up in its clutches, it is hard to leave. Liberation is to never be caught up in anything.

3. REAL LIFE IS NOT REAL

A performer disciple was telling Babaji about *abhinaya*, or the art of acting and how it communicates.
Babaji: And what about *abhinaya* or enactment of situations in real life? That is also acting and enactment. Real life is also not real.

4. THE SHIFTING PHENOMENON OF EXISTENCE

D: Babaji, whenever I leave home and hearth and come to meet you, people tell me that they would never do such a reckless thing, because their feet are firmly planted on the ground.
Babaji: Ask them, which ground? In this shifting phenomenon of Existence, where is the firm ground on which you can plant your feet?

---

1 The 'D' in all conversations refers to Disciple.

5. 'AISH KARO'

Disciples stricken by worry and anxiety would constantly unburden in front of Babaji and end by saying, 'Babaji, what should I do?'

Babaji: Do nothing. *Aish karo*. Not *'aish'* in the sense of giving in to excesses or indulging, as is normally understood, but the *'aish'* that comes from *'esha'* or *Shiva* / Master. Abide in *Shiva* or be a Master - that is what is meant by *'aish karo'*.

6. RISE ABOVE CIRCUMSTANCES

D: Babaji, my mother-in-law is really getting on my nerves!

Babaji (laughing): Why don't you just wink at her?

D(another one): Babaji my mother-in-law is also getting on my nerves.

Babaji (laughing): Why don't you give her a nice, tight pinch! Jokes apart, what I mean is that you must learn to rise above the trivialities of life. Where practical solutions are possible, implement them. Where no such solution presents itself, ignore the problem, put it aside in your mind and try to transcend it.

A *sadhaka* has to rise above all negative and bothersome situations that often have only nuisance value.

7. LETTING GO OF THE PAST

D: Babaji, my mother-in-law stresses me out completely with her nagging.

Babaji: Where is she now?

D: At home.

Babaji: And where are you now?

D: Here.

Babaji: Let me tell you a story –

Two monks were crossing a river. The river was swollen with rainwater and was difficult to ferry. A young lady stood helplessly on the shore, wondering how to go across. One of

the monks offered to carry her across.
Having reached the other shore, he put her down.
After travelling some distance, the other monk said, "Brother you should not have carried that woman."
The monk replied, "Oh, I put her down an hour back, but you seem to be still carrying her!"

8. CASTING AWAY STALE MEMORIES

To a disciple who was brooding -
Babaji: The inner life has to be managed in much the same way as the outer life.
You sweep the house daily, you dust the furniture, you bring fresh milk, fruits and vegetables for your daily use; and then why do you preserve age-old ideas in your mind? Let your thoughts be fresh too. (To another disciple who was a dancer) Let your thoughts be fresh, graceful, and full of joy and beauty like the dance.

9. RISING ABOVE SENTIMENT

A disciple was sulking in one corner.
Babaji: Hello, why are you sulking?
D: Because you were angry with me yesterday.
Babaji (laughing): But that was yesterday and you still remember it? When will you rise above silly sentiment and self importance.Nothing can be achieved by those who give undue importance to their petty sentiments.
(chanting his favourite *shloka* from the *Avadhoota Gita.*)
प्रमादेन न संदेहः किं करिष्यामि वृत्तिमान्
उत्पद्यन्ते विलीयन्ते बुदबुदाश्च यथा जले ॥
As bubbles arise and dissolve in water, psychological states come and go. What can sentimental souls who identify with these illusive states, ever hope to achieve?

10. WHY ME ?

A disciple was dejected because unexpected bad weather had disrupted a very prestigious show that she was to have.

D: Babaji, why did this have to happen to me?

Babaji: Then, to whom should it have happened?

11. BABAJI, WHAT WOULD YOU DO IN MY PLACE ?

A disciple was very hassled about many personal problems and was discussing it with Babaji. After much discussion, no solution seemed to emerge and in exasperation she said –

D: Babaji, what would you do in my place?

Babaji: Oh, I can never be in your place. Thinking along these lines, we waste much energy in empty imaginations. 'If', 'would have', 'should have', and 'could have', are all empty thoughts. They may help you understand a situation, but they can never help you to find a solution to problems.

12. NEVER COVET THESE

Babaji (to a disciple who was crying): *Beta,* these tears are to be shed for others not for one's self. Those who cry for themselves waste vital energies in the process. Honour, respect and tears are for others. Never covet them for yourself.

13. INNER EMPTINESS

D: Babaji, that girl is all-alone in this world, with nobody to support her.

Babaji: How can she be alone and supportless? She has her Self, her mind, body and her Conciousness always with her. It is because we live outside our Self, that we feel a sense of want and lack.

14. THE DIVINE WILL

To a disciple who was sad and complaining-

Babaji: Whatever is, is for the best - *jo hai, jaisa hai, badhiya hai.*

Because whatever is, is due to Her will - *jo hai, bhagvati ki iccha se hai.*

If friends desert you, that is Her wish. If success eludes you, that is for the best. (Laughing) Why, even if you have bad breath and it puts people off, that is also for the best. Now you can sit in peace and worship God!

15. TAKE WHAT IS YOUR LOT IN LIFE

While trekking in the Himalayas, disciples would be famished by the end of the day, because budgets were very strict with Babaji and food was measured.

At the end of a tiresome trek, a famished disciple lunged for the *chapatis.* Seeing that the one on top was burnt, she adroitly pulled out the one underneath...but not before Babaji's sharp gaze caught her...

Babaji: (angrily): For whom have you left the burnt *chapati*? Take what is in your lot, in the course of life. By avoiding unpleasant situations, you delay and interfere with the workings of your *karma.*

16. WHATEVER BHAGAVATI DOES IS FOR THE BEST

A single S.T. bus connected the *ashram* to Lonavla, the nearest city. The bus was far from punctual and often did not turn up at all. The scheduled time was more a wish, than reality. However, if we missed that bus, we were jailed in the jungle for one more day, with no means of communication, as the *ashram* did not even have a phone! In fact, this erratic S.T. bus has taught many a disciple, simple lessons in non-attachment from family and work, living with whatever is, the futility of worrying, and understanding that Life can go on without their esteemed presence.

D: (Exasperatedly walking back from the bus-stop, having missed the bus.) Babaji, I have missed the bus, it has gone!

Babaji: (Laughing): *ghar ke buddhu ghar ko laute* – O, our dear foolish ones have returned home'. Just yesterday, you were saying that you wanted to spend your whole life at the *ashram*! See how kind *Bhagavati* is. She has gifted you at least one more day's stay at the *ashram*!

D: Huh! I have an important appointment, my child is waiting for me, and a number of pending chores have to be completed at home before I resume work tomorrow...

Babaji: Whatever *Bhagavati* does, is for the best.

Listen to this story -

Emperor Akbar and his witty minister Birbal were once going on a hunt. The emperor hurt his finger on the way and looked towards Birbal for sympathy. Birbal said, "Oh Sire, whatever happens, happens for the best." Akbar was livid with rage - to first of all be in pain and then to be sermonized by a mere minister. "Go and stand in that empty well", he ordered Birbal, in anger. So saying, he continued on his hunt, leaving Birbal standing in the well.

At some distance, Akbar met tribals who were performing a ritual offering to their Goddess. They were delighted to see the Emperor, as they needed some human flesh to offer to their Goddess. Capturing the king, they started to prepare for the ritual.

The king was asked to undress, as they needed to scrutinize whether his body was whole, intact, and fit for ritual offering. Relieved, the king quickly drew their attention to his bruised, broken and bleeding finger. The tribals immediately let go off the Emperor, realizing that he was not an apt sacrifice.

Happy, but ashamed, Akbar hastened to meet Birbal; to tell him his tale and beg forgiveness for not understanding the wisdom of his words. He rushed to pull his beloved minister out of the well and embraced him with tears of repentance. As they walked back to the palace, suddenly the king enquired, "Oh, Birbal, it is true that my little accident saved me from death; but what good did standing in a well, in the scorching sun, do to you?" Birbal said, "Oh, King can't you see that, if I had accompanied you on the hunt, the tribals would have considered offering my body instead of yours. Since my body is blemish free, for sure, I would have been slaughtered! That little, humiliating punishment that you gave me, has indeed been a blessing in disguise!"

Babaji continued - It is difficult to understand the workings of that Higher Intelligence. It is easier, and within our capacity to simply cultivate an acceptance of that Higher Intelligence.

(It is needless to add that, in his compassion and kindness, Babaji always made that extra day spent at the *ashram*, a day worth remembering with his love and sharing of Truth. We would go away feeling - 'Whatever *Bhagavati* does is for the best.')

17. NATURE LOOKS AFTER EVERYONE

D: Babaji, I really want to come to your *ashram*, but where can I leave my child?

Babaji: Why, you can leave him under that tree! Nature looks after everyone. You think that the world moves around only because of your efforts.

18. NOTHING IS USELESS IN NATURE'S PLAN

D: Babaji, do *bhoots* (ghosts) exist?

Babaji: If there is a name; there must be a corresponding form. This world is only a play of name and form. They are two sides of the same coin. All things have a name, a form and qualities. Therefore, all things have a use. Even things that we discard as useless, have some use. For example, did you know that the placenta that covers the child is a very useful thing? If rubbed on the child's and the mother's body, the skin will remain smooth and no unwanted hair will grow on the body.

For example even things like a tiger's claws, a cat's placenta etc. have great value. In Nature, no plant, no flower, no stone, nothing is useless. *Ayurveda,* and even the sciences of magic, are a proof of this fact.

Do you know the story of a great *ayurveda* master who wanted to take a final exam of his student? He asked him to go find a herb that had no use. The student spent days together in the jungle and came back disappointed having failed to find such a herb. Happily, the *guru* patted him on the back and said – "You have learnt well."

Similarly, there are no useless human beings. Everyone has a role to fulfil, a talent that makes him significant in Nature's scheme of things.

19. EACH ONE IS UNIQUE

An artist: (praising his *guru)* O, he is one of a kind, one in a million!

Babaji (to the artist): So are you. Each human being is unique.

20. CAN I CALL HOME?

A disciple had come to spend a couple of days with Babaji.

D: Babaji, can I just call home and find out how things are?

Babaji: No. *Bhagvati* will look after them.

21. DEALING WITH 'KAMAVASANA'

D: But Babaji, what does one do with *'kamavasana'* or lust and desire?

Babaji: First of all, do not look upon it as an enemy. Do not oppose it or fight with it. If it arises, let it; do not obstruct it. Look at it with love and understanding and chide it gently – 'this body is God's. You will get nothing from this body; there is no place for you here.' – If a dog comes to your door repeatedly, but you do not feed it, it is going to give up one day. The same is the case with *kama vasana.*

When the *vasana* arises, calm it – wash your hands and feet and drink a couple of glasses of water. Kama is a form of agni or fire and needs to be cooled down and water is a coolant. Even this simple little ritual, will help cope with *kama vasanas* and allow the reckless impulse to pass over.

These six enemies *(shadripus)* or feelings of lust *(kama)*, anger *(krodha)*, greed *(lobha)*, delusion *(moha)*, intoxication *(mada)*, hate *(matsara)* are 'guests' of the body. Let go off them lovingly. They have come for a feast of the *panchavishayas* or objects of the world. Tell them, that these cannot be found in the pure body that belongs to the gods. Let them go with love, if you suppress and control them, they will resurge with even greater violence.

A deep and fearless understanding of the nature of lust and desire, and an intelligent, far-sighted awareness of their cause and effects alone can assauge the enemies within. An enemy befriended is better than an enemy conquered.

22. LUST IS AS GOOD AS THE SEX ACT

Once Babaji saw a person greedily eyeing sarees and jewellery.

Babaji: Ah, there she is ready to enjoy the sexual act. All lusting is an expression of the sex act. The sexual act is not only with the opposite sex. It is engaged in, each time you lust and desire. This wonder called the world, comes into being through sex i.e. lusting. This coming in and going out, from one birth to another, is the primary expression of the sexual act.

23. SEXUAL EXCESSES

D: (seeing a row of donkeys at the *dhobi ghat*): Babaji, these poor donkeys are always abused and insulted. Their very name has become a curse word.

Babaji: Their fault is sexual indiscrimination. That one trait can destroy a person and cause loss of intelligence. It is for this reason that a donkey, is looked down upon.

24. ON MARRIAGE

D: Babaji, I don't understand this institution of marriage.

Babaji: Let me tell you a joke –

A man went to his guru and said, "Guruji, I have found a girl to marry." The *guru* said, "Now, my son, you are of no use to me." After some days the disciple returned and said, "*Guruji*, now I am married." The *Guru* said, "Now you are of no use to yourself." After some time the disciple returned and said, "*Guruji*, now I have children."

"Now", said the *Guru* laughing, "you are of no use at all !"

D: So is marriage so bad?

Babaji: No. But you have to understand two things. Firstly, that not everyone is made for marriage. But our society pushes everyone into it. Secondly, if two people have to grow within it and evolve spiritually, then the level of awareness of the partners has to be high. It has to be seen as a marriage of *Shiva* and *Shakti*. For others, in the name of love, it is only a 'pin-cushion' effect, like all worldly relationships.

D: What is that?

Babaj: The cushion is the comfort and the sweet, sweet things that the relationship seems to provide, but actually you are only being pricked all the time. In marriage as in everything else, conscious awareness is all that matters - and it has to be present on both sides. Only thus can true love and joy blossom.

25. LOVE AND ATTACHMENT

D: Babaji, what is the difference between love and attachment?

Babaji: Where love results in pain, know that it is not love, but attachment.

26 . HOW TO TREAT A WOMAN

Visitor: Babaji, my wife is always unhappy with me.

Babaji: A woman is like a *veena* - a stringed instrument. You have to know how to tune the *veena* and then play it.

27. LOVE AND PHYSICAL EXPRESSION

A disciple was kissing her child many times to express love and affection.

Babaji: Too much physical expression of love is not good. It only increases attachment and sentimentality.

28. INTEGRATION OF HEAD AND HEART

Babaji could often sharply reprimand a disciple to bring home the point that, a *sadhaka* has to take full responsibility for his life. Belief in grace and an attitude of humility and surrender are no substitute for courageous responsibility.

D(disgruntled): Babaji, my marriage is in a mess. Now you alone can find a way out for me. I leave everything in your hands. Only your grace can save me.

Babaji: Well, you chose to marry him not I, so go ahead and find the way out. *Bhagvati* has given you a mind and intelligence, go ahead and put it to proper use. When you need to use the head, you use the heart. When you need to use the heart, you use the head and when you need to use both, you do not use either. Then, in this state of utter confusion, you suddenly want to surrender to *Bhagavati*. Do you think this surrender is a child's play? It requires the highest integration of the head and heart.

29. WHY SUFFERING

Visitor: Babaji, what is wrong in living with my preferences, prejudices and cravings? That is life, isn't it?

Babaji: Sure, but that is the path to unhappiness. You may choose it if you wish to, but it will cause suffering. You know the *Buddha* has said, "The root of all suffering is craving,
The root of all craving is desire,
The root of all desire is ignorance."

Ignorance makes you preserve your preferences, prejudices and cravings. You are the inheritor of unalloyed, uninterrupted and unconditional joy but if you want to settle for the bitter/ sweet, fleeting happiness, go ahead. It is your life.

30. ON DESIRE

D: Babaji, now I don't have many desires, just one desire...
Babaji (laughing): Oh, you can have many children from one wife!

31. BHAVA, ABHAVA & SVABHAVA

D: Babaji, I cannot deny that when my desires are fulfilled, I am happy and when they are unfulfilled, I am unhappy. So, is that not natural and should one not just live with that reality?
Babaji: In life, there is always going to be *'bhava'* or fulfillment of a desire, and *'abhava'* or non-fulfillment of a desire. Life is a tussle between these two, but there is a third vital factor. How do you react to the fate of your desires? That brings to light your *'svabhava'* or intrinsic nature and if deeply pondered upon it will reveal your eternal nature.

Svabhava, can be understood as your personality. And beyond it, is your Eternal Nature. You must first understand the anatomy of your preferences, prejudices *(agrahas)* and concepts or thoughts that make up your *svabhava,* and when by a clear understanding they drop off, you will see your *mula svabhava* or Eternal Nature.

32. SHUNNING NEGATIVITY

Babaji: Stay away from *duhkha* (negativity), arguments, mental stress, offensive thoughts and people, worldly talk and inane conversation.

A *sadhaka* especially, must consciously and thoughtfully stay away from these.

33. NEGATIVE THINKING

Babaji(to a disciple who was prone to negative thinking.):

See, this life is like a ration queue. If you stand in line for sugar, you will get sugar. If you stand in line for kerosene, you will get kerosene. If you stand in line for negativity, negativity will come to you. If you stand in a queue for positivity, that will come to you.

There are 64,000 crore positive forces in the universe. Why don't you queue up for those. You know, that is why Bhagavati is described as, 'One who is served by 64,000 crore *yoginis*' *(mahacatushasthikoti yoginigana sevita)*

34. THREE BOONS WASTED

Babaji: Even *Shiva* cannot help those who are intensely and persistently negative. Let me tell you a story - Once there was a couple that was violently negative and antagonistic to each other. One day, they were engaged in a heated argument when *Shiva* and *Parvati* happened to pass by. Seeing their plight, *Parvati* begged her Lord to help them. *Shiva* warned her that they are beyond help, but she persisted.

So he went to them and said, "I give each of you a boon. Ask whatever you want."

In a fit of anger, the husband asked that his wife be converted into a pig. He then asked the wife what she wanted.

Vengefully she spat out, "Let him also become a pig."

Then, *Shiva* turned to their little child and asked, "And my child, what would you like to do with your boon?"

Sobbing, the child said, "Make them who they were before!"

Babaji continued: So you see, even three boons from *Shiva* himself, failed to ameliorate their lives.

35. NEVER FIGHT

A disciple who was engaged in a heated altercation with someone, was explaining to Babaji that he did not mean to fight but...

Babaji: Never fight or get involved in heated arguments. If such an occasion presents itself, just extricate yourself from it and consciously move away.

36. WHY WORRY ?

To a disciple eaten up by worry-

Babaji: Precious life force is lost in worry. No good can ever come of worry. Meaningless, ceaseless, confused thinking, depression and dejection rob the mind of precious, subtle energies, that are needed to achieve single-mindedness or *ekagrata.* Worry and other such destructive, dissipating thoughts, come in the way of reaching a meditative state. Nothing sucks the body off subtle energies and causes it to waste as worry. Never entertain worries. Always keep yourself in a state of calm joy.

D: And how does one do that?

Babaji: First of all, you must learn to lessen your expectations from others and from life. Expectations are the root of sorrow. Nobody is obliged to you for anything.

There are two other practical ways of staying free of anxiety. Whatever action needs to be taken, take it, and where no course of action seems possible, allow things to be. That is all. Do what has to be 'done', and leave it at that, in the hands of *Bhagavati.*

37. FIND YOUR PEACE FIRST

D: Babaji, yesterday I was trying to understand the problems of some people and the day passed in that way. The day before, some friends had come to unburden, and later in the night, my family demanded my attention …

Babaji: My *Gurumaharaj* used to say, "This world is like a forest on fire. Save your limbs and run." You cannot afford to waste time giving peace of mind to others when you have not found your own.

38. THE HUMAN PLIGHT

D: Babaji, look at that poor cockroach!

Babaji: Well, it is not any poorer than you are. In fact, the human being and the human plight are most pitiable. Your deceitful, self-important mind, trapped in psychological time (past and future), and fixed notions, gives you no peace. The overuse, abuse and misuse of the human mind has killed natural and spontaneous living.

Due to perversion, the greatest blessing (i.e. the human mind) has become a tragic curse.

39. RENOUNCE INSISTENCES

D: Babaji, I don't like the way my children behave and if only my husband would do as I say...

Babaji: It is these *agrahas,* these preferences, prejudices, concepts and fixed patterns of thinking that make one unhappy in life. Why don't you just renounce them? If that is too difficult for you, why don't you just give them to me?

40. ON CRITICIZING

Once a disciple was criticizing someone.

Babaji (sternly): My dear, the way you perceive that person is entirely subjective. It is not the whole Truth. It is a limited, petty opinion, and a reaction of your egotistical mind. This world comes into being because of your mind.

D: Babaji, what do you mean by my mind?

Babaji: I mean the sum total of your preferences, prejudices, likes, dislikes, stale memories of past experience and concepts of morality, ideals and all the ideas that make you take a 'stand' on matters.When this mind dies, your world also dies. And then you will be able to see the world as it is, in God. You will then stop evaluating, judging and criticizing people, and in turn be unaffected by their evaluation and criticism.

41. EXPECTATIONS

D: Babaji, familiarity with people brings disappointment.

Babaji: It is not the familiarity, but your own expectations that bring disappointment.

42. GIVE UP GRASPING AND LEAVING

D (triumphantly): Babaji, now I have finally given up smoking.

Babaji: If you give up something, you will also take up something. Try to go beyond grasping and leaving. You must bring about fundamental changes in the level of your consciousness. Otherwise, it is like pruning a tree. In no time the leaves will grow back and once again, it will need pruning. You have to burn the very seed of this tree of *samsara*.

Let me tell you a story - A man had come to a *guru* to understand the Truth. The *guru* asked him to carry out a task, before he started teaching him. He said, "See that pile of knotted thread there. Just undo the knots for me." The disciple started in all earnesty but no sooner had he undone one knot, another one would form. After many such efforts, he realized that there was no point in doing the exercise, as the bundle was hopelessly entangled. In exasperation, he just threw the bundle of thread into the fire. The *guru* looked on in amusement and said, 'Well learnt!'

Babaji continued: The dualistic mind is caught between good and bad, right and wrong and therefore accepts and rejects. However, no real progress can be made on the spiritual path with this method. This way you will always remain in bondage.

(Babaji chanting away in a state of deep inwardness)

यदा नाहं तदा मोक्षो यदाहं बंधनं तदा ।
मत्वेति हेलया किञ्चिन्मा गृहाण विमुञ्च मा ॥

D: What does that mean?

Babaji: Where there is no *aham* (egotistical 'I'), there is liberation.Where there is the *aham* (ego), there is bondage. Knowing this fact, refrain from accepting or rejecting anything.

D: And how does one do that?
Babaji: By identifying with that Supreme Self and not with this mind- body complex, with its likes and dislikes, acceptances and rejections. Have no sense of accomplishment or dejection in the habits of this mind-body complex. Simply be a witness to it.

Remember that name of our Goddess, *'heyopadeyavarjita'* – She has nothing to reject or accept. The enlightened one neither accepts nor rejects anything. These 1000 names of The Goddess are forms of your own Consciousness; never forget that. Apply them to your daily life and you will become *sakshat Bhagavati,* a living goddess.

43. FEAR AND AGGRESSION

D: Babaji, that person is very aggressive and frightening. She makes me afraid of her. I cannot handle it.
Babaji: It is a law of Nature, that only those animals who are afraid, try to frighten others. Trying to frighten others is a defense mechanism. Have sympathy for such people. They suffer their fears manifold more than you. Also, remember that you are frightened because there is fear in you. Nobody can 'make' you afraid.

44. CROSSING THE OCEAN OF LIFE

A disciple's heart was heavy with dejection.
Babaji: My dear, only they can successfully cross this *samsara sagara* (ocean of life), who can be light like a twig of straw, free from the weight of their opinions, preferences, prejudices, achievements and ambitions, sorrows and frustrations.

45. INNER CHIMNEY

A disciple had just installed a small chimney over the gas in her kitchen. It was meant to absorb all the impure fumes and keep the air clean.

Babaji: I like the concept of a chimney. We must create a chimney inside us.

46. STRESS RELIEF

Babaji (after reading an article on stress relief): You know, people are stressed because they think only of themselves.

47. NOBODY WANTS GOD

Babaji, sharing his views on people who had visited him and were full of their woes -

Babaji: Nobody wants God. Everyone wants the sweet, sweet *(meetha, meetha)* things of life.

48. SHARE THE GOOD THINGS OF LIFE

D: Babaji, I feel like eating up all the chocolates I have.

Babaji: No. Always share the good things of life. Never keep them solely for your enjoyment.

Let me tell you a story –

Once the gods and the demons were invited for a feast. They were allowed to eat as much as they wanted, but on one condition – while eating, they should not bend their arms at the elbow. The demons were perplexed at this strange condition and helplessly sat staring at the food.The gods however, lined themselves in rows facing each other and picking up the morsels of food, fed each other!

In another story, the Gods, demons and humans went to *Brahma* for guidance. He simply uttered the syllable *'da'*. Pressed for an explanation he said, for the gods, *'da'* stands for *'dama'* or continence as they were self indulgent; for the demons, the *'da'* was reflective of *'daya'* or compassion as they were violent and cruel; for the humans, the *'da'* was indicative of *'dana'* or charity and sharing.

49. EAT WITH ALL YOUR FINGERS

Babaji (to a disciple who was trying to eat daintily):
Use all the five fingers while eating. The fingers release digestive juices when they are used for eating. Besides, that isolated finger shows the divisiveness in you. Try to be whole and gathered, in whatever you do.

50. TASTY FOOD

A child was hogging some dish that he loved.
Babaji: My son, do not run after taste. Beware of it. Eat simple food to your heart's content; but practice restraint when offered tasty, fancy food.

51. OVEREATING

A disciple was prone to overeating.
Babaji: My son, gluttony is not a good thing. Indiscipline of any one sense organ, will lead to indiscipline of all the others. If your desire for food is insatiable and huge, it will be the same with your desire for sex and wealth.

52. DO IT WITH YOUR WHOLE BEING

To a disciple who was reading while eating.
Babaji: Never read while eating. Whatever you do, do it single mindedly, with your whole being.

53. EAT CONSCIOUSLY

Babaji: *Arre laddu,*(sweet heart) how often have I told you not to eat while reading?
D: Why Babaji?
Babaji: Because food needs and deserves all your attention. Chewing the food is very important. This is possible only if you are attentive. When you chew the food, it mixes with the saliva and becomes energised because this saliva has rejuvenating properties.

The subtlest elements of the food you eat go on to make and nourish the mind, the less subtle elements go on to form your blood and the gross part of the food goes on to create flesh and bones. Thus, you are what you eat. If you eat mindlessly, you will chew carelessly. When that happens, the body cannot extract the nourishment from the food.

Infact, how you eat is even more important than what you eat. You see, just as when you study, you absorb only in proportion to your level of attentiveness. So also, the attentiveness with which you eat will determine the extent to which your inner systems are able to absorb the life force from the food. If eaten attentively, the same amount of food will give you much more energy. Talking, watching TV, reading or doing any other activity while eating, is harmful.

In fact, whatever you do, try to do single-mindedly and with full attention. That is why we say, '*dhyan se karo* - perform acts in a state of full attentiveness.' Whether you are rolling *chapattis,* sweeping the floor, doing more intricate or intellectual work, maintain a state of unbroken attentiveness and you may not need to practice formal meditation. Besides, food is *Bhagavati*. The least you can do is pay her respect by being mindful as you eat.

D: Babaji, I understand, but please let me keep this one habit of reading while eating.

Babaji (laughing): O, you are welcome to keep all your habits. I only point the way to happiness, ease and awareness. The final choice is yours.

54. NON-VEGETARIAN FOODS

D: Babaji, is there anything wrong in eating non-vegetarian food?

Babaji: *ham jo bhi indriyaun se grahan karte hai vaisehi ho jate hai, vaisahi hamara svabhav ho jata hai* – Our nature is shaped by whatever our senses hold or absorb. Now, if you apply this truth to the food you eat, then it means that you become what you eat. Unlike plants, we cannot make our own food. We therefore need to get it from outside. Both plants and animals are living, but plants don't have *vasanas,* lusts, or cravings. Their nature is to give. Therefore, if you eat plants, fruits etc. their non-violent and generous nature will be ingested by you. On the contrary, if you eat animals, who are always full of *vasanas* and aggression you will absorb these. In the past, the *kshatriyas,* or the warrior class, who had to fight battles, needed this kind of aggression and so for them it was alright to consume non-vegetarian food. However, for others this is not true. Non-vegetarian food involves violence to the life of vulnerable and helpless beings. If you cannot create life, what gives you the right to take it away? If you are not able to gain merit, at least do not go around collecting de-merit by killing. When fruits, vegetables and grains are available, why do you want to traumatise innocent creatures? They are bound to curse you.

For a *sadhaka* especially, non-vegetarian food is positively harmful. The positive vibrations of *mantra sadhana* will never accrue in a house where non-vegetarian food is consumed.

55. UNTOUCHED BY HAND

Babaji (reading the instructions on a food packet): 'Untouched by hand'. (Laughing) *Arre* these people are *laddoos.* What transforms things is the touch of the human hand. The human hand can energise everything. These antiseptic foods will do nothing for your growth. You know, in our tradition, when a *sadhaka,* is undertaking important *sadhanas,* he only eats food cooked by the *guru.*

56. ON WASTAGE

A child, who had some leftovers on his plate, went and put it in the wash-basin.

Babaji: Who has wasted this food? Let him do without food for a few days. Whatever you waste, you will lack in life. If you waste money, you will be short of money. If you waste time, you will lack time. Nature gives in abundance, but because we waste, we lack.

57. THE SENSE OF PROPORTION

A disciple was given to putting too much chilly in the food.

Babaji: My son, a sense of *pramana* (proportion and discretion) is the most important thing in life. Those who lack that, miss the Truth.

58. EATING IN HOTELS

Babaji (to a disciple): Try not to eat 'out' too much.

D: Why?

Babaji: Food sold in hotels is prepared to make money and not to nourish you. Too much eating 'out' will not only ruin your health, but will also grip you with that same mercenary tendency.

59. ON BEING IMPRESSED

D: Babaji, I was impressed by that person's command over the *shastras.*

Babaji: If you are impressed with anything, know that you are still a slave and not a master.

60. LAZINESS

Babaji (to a lazy disciple): Time should not be wasted in lazing around. Look at me, I engage myself in simple acts of day-to-day life and perform them with care. If not, I read and enrich myself. Time wasted, is dissipation of opportunities offered by destiny.

61. LOLLING IN BED

Babaji: Why are you lolling in bed?

D: Just like that Babaji; enjoying my holiday.
Babaji: Never loll in bed. Either sleep deeply or get up and go about your work. If you loll around you will become a *bhogi* and the lust in you will increase.

62. THE IMPORTANCE OF CLEAN FEET

Babaji: Look at those dirty feet of yours!
D: Does it matter?
Babaji: Yes, of course. If you have dirty unkempt feet, your mind can never be clean and calm. Vital nerve centers are located in the feet, and are in turn, connected to centers in the brain. A *yogi's* feet must be like a baby's. That is why, all our gods and goddesses are known to have feet that are soft and pure like a lotus.

63. CLOSE THE CIRCUIT OF THE BODY

To a disciple who was sitting with his legs spread out.
Babaji: Never spread your legs like that. Always close the circuit of the body so as not to dissipate energies. Especially while meditating, you must close all the circuits of the body and seal energies, in order to redirect them upwards.

64. AVOID NERVOUS TWITCHING

To a disciple who was shaking his leg nervously-
Babaji: Shaking the legs and feet nervously is a very common problem. It seems insignificant, but tremendous essential energies are lost in such a mindless activity.

65. WHAT ARE YOU READING?

Babaji (to a fellow traveler): What are you reading?
Traveller : A murder mystery.
Babaji: If you read about murder, then someday you may commit murder. Be careful what you read and the thoughts that you plant in your head. A *sadhaka* especially, must stay

away from frivolous, negative literature and other such forms of entertainment.

66. INTELLECTUAL TALK IS OF NO USE

To a young college student who could talk very intellectually and cleverly.

Babaji: Tell me what you can 'do'. What can you do with your hands? Can you cook, can you draw, or can you build a house? Mere intellectual talk and understanding is of no use.

67. BE MINDFUL AT ALL TIMES

Babaji was cooking and spilt the gravy while stirring it.

Babaji: Ah, this is lack of awareness. One must be careful and mindful of the slightest loss of awareness.

68. MINDLESS ACTIVITY

On seeing a child aimlessly throwing a ball around.

Babaji: My dear, any game that you play, should help you to develop a skill. It must inculcate self-discipline. Not only are mindless games a waste of time, but they can blunt your intelligence and even become a habit. All play should help in developing some skill and inculcate intelligence. Infact, everything you do should be perfectly mindful.

(Babaji himself displayed great mindfulness in whatever he did. Even the most ordinary activity of peeling an apple, became an art when he did it. He would make sure that the peel came off as a single, spiraling piece. It would be thin and as close to the surface of the fruit as possible; as, he would explain, all the essential nutrients of the fruit are just below the skin.When carrying out any task with such involvement, his breath would slow down, becoming almost imperceptible and a peace and quiet would surround him).

69. THIS IS NOT SAMARPAN

A disciple was neglecting herself completely, being caught in familial duties, so much so that she found very little time to even look after her bodily needs.

Babaji: You have to understand that you owe something to yourself.

Tu hai to tera sansar hai. Jee hai to jahan hai – if you exist, the world exists. Indian women have been really doing great injustice to themselves in the name of '*samarpan*' (surrender). In the name of selflessness, they have committed a grave crime against their very selves.

This life is for your growth and evolution. If your so-called 'selflessness' does not allow that to happen, then it is only a form of suicide. This compulsion to be nice and morally good has sapped the inner strength of our women.

70. VILLAGERS V/S URBANITES

Watching peasants in the *ashram* village, working and struggling for mere survival –

Babaji: They are killed by their bodily needs while the urban city dweller is killed by his mind.

71. 100% CONFIDENCE

Babaji: Be attentive at all times, to all things in life.

Unless you have 100% confidence, do not undertake anything.

72. TO ERR IS HUMAN

Babaji: One who never errs is God.

He who errs once is human,

He who errs twice is an ordinary human being,

He who errs thrice is a fool.

A human being should make use of his life-experience and intelligence, while working.

73. FREEDOM

Babaji would often come home with small gifts that he would receive from friends and disciples and would show them off with pride and joy. He would always make it a point to gloat over the fact that they were for free!

D: Babaji, you are lucky to get these things for free. We poor householders have to earn every bit of our livelihood.

Babaji: When you will be Free, you will also get everything for free.

74. WHAT AM I THERE FOR ?

Babaji was pointing out to the harmonious qualities in a disciple.

D: Babaji, won't all this praise go to my head?

Babaji: It is essential to dispassionately assess one's qualities, the positive as well as the negative ones.

D: Why?

Babaji: So that, you keep the good ones while trying to throw off the bad ones. If you are not aware of your good qualities, they might also be thrown away. To know yourself means to know everything about yourself.

D: And what if I become puffed up with pride at all the compliments?

Babaji: What am I there for? I know how to take care of that too!

75. DADAJI HAS NOT GONE ANYWHERE

A disciple had lost her father, who also happened to be a very dear friend of Babaji's. That day Babaji happened to visit the disciple. He was unaware of the demise.

Babaji: So, how is my dear friend Dadaji?

D: He is no more.

Babaji (without any change in expression): Oh! is that so? That must be *Bhagavati's* wish. How are you?

The disciple just looked at him with tear-filled eyes.
Babaji: Oh you mad cap, why are you crying? Dadaji has not gone anywhere. (Pointing to the empty glass in which she had offered him water). Only the glass has broken. Its contents have in fact, only spread far and near. Now Dadaji is everywhere, far and near, closer to you than ever before. Only his body has passed away.

76. THE GURU WITHIN

D: Babaji, sometimes it is very confusing when different people give conflicting advice on a given situation. What should one do?
Babaji: Once, *Shiva* and *Parvati* were travelling with their bull *Nandi*. *Shiva* was seated on the bull, while *Parvati* walked alongside.
Some passers by commented, 'Look at that shameless man, he rides a bull while the poor lady accompanies on foot!'
Embarrassed, *Shiva* let *Parvati* ride the bull. Again, there was a comment, 'What an immodest woman, her Lord, the great *Shiva* walks and she has no shame in riding the bull.'
The divine couple bow down to public opinion and decide to walk with the bull by their side till they hear peels of ridiculing laughter. 'What a stupid couple', say the villagers. 'Here they have a fine mount and like fools they tire themselves out!'
Babaji continued: You can't win with the world. Don't seek the approval of the world. Do what has to be done. That's all.
D: But how Babaji?
Babaji: Be your own guide or *guru*.
D: How?
Babaji: Awaken the inner *guru* and learn to distinguish it from your deceptive, greedy and approval-seeking mind.

77. LOVE IS THE ESSENCE

D: Babaji, I want to have a daughter.

Babaji: Can you not adopt me as your daughter?
D: Please Babaji, I want a cute little daughter whom I can dress up in pigtails and frilly clothes. I cannot express myself that way with a balding Babaji!
Babaji: Love is the essence. Man, woman, child, the aged, these are only forms. Why try to grasp these changing forms? Go to the essence.

78. I TOO AM JUST A TRAVELER

Babaji: Why don't you stay for a few more days at the *ashram?*
D: But I only have clothes for 2-3 days.
Babaji: What you need for 2-3 days is what you need for a lifetime.
Let me tell you a story –
A man went to meet a *Sufi* saint. As he entered the saint's house, he was surprised to see that all it contained was a jug of water and a mat to sleep on.
"Is this all that you possess?" asked the visitor, surprised.
"Why, you too have only this small bag that you are carrying," replied the saint.
"O, that is because I am travelling." said the visitor.
"I too am just a traveler", said the saint.

79. CONSCIOUS CHANGE

D: Babaji ever since I have met you, I have changed a lot.
Babaji: Change is inevitable and bound to happen. What is important is the direction in which the change has taken place. More importantly, whether the change is conscious or unconscious.

80. DOES YOUR HOUSE BELONG TO YOU ?

D (angry with some one in the family): Babaji, this house belongs to me. At least here, I have a right to assert myself.
Babaji: Does this house belong to you?

Once, a *Sufi* saint was resting in the courtyard of the palace and happened to block the path of emperor *Akbar*. When asked to get up, he said, "Why don't you just allow me to rest for awhile in this caravan?" The Emperor said, in anger "Old man, you dare call this a caravan. Don't you know, this is my palace?"

"Is it?" asked the saint. "Who lived here before you?"

"Why, my father", said the Emperor.

" And who lived here before him?" asked the saint.

" Well, if you had any common sense, you would know that his father and then his father and his father and so on..." said the impatient Monarch.

"O, King, a place that has served as a resting place for so many down the years, can only be a makeshift shelter or caravan. How can it be yours?"

Babaji continued: *Gurumaharaj* used to say, *"sab apne hai, aur kuch bhi apna nahi hain"* – Everyone belongs to you, but nothing is yours.

81. WHAT SHOULD BE REMEMBERED

D: Babaji, I could not sleep the whole of last night because I lost a watch worth Rs.1500.

Babaji: O, once while travelling by train, I had also lost a watch with diamonds in it, worth Rs.2500. But I slept very well that night, because I immediately forgot about it. Loss of valuables (material things) should be forgotten, but loss of values should be remembered or pondered over.

82. BEWARE OF MATERIAL TRAPPINGS

D: Babaji, can I have my *rudraksha mala* strung in gold?

Babaji: Why? What is wrong with the present silver threading? Beware of material trappings and greed for possessions.

83. BEWARE OF COMFORTS

Babaji (seeing some children being pampered by their

parents): Beware of comforts. These comforts soften and weaken the mind. Children raised in too much comfort will be weak and lacking in real courage.

84. GOOD GROOMING V/S FASHION

Babaji (to a disciple): Why are you so sloppily dressed? Our *Bhagavati* is always well groomed.

Babaji(to another disciple): Oh, I see that you have adorned yourself with buckles and hair clips and what not! Being well groomed does not mean being fashionable. A *sadhaka* should not run after fashion.

85. BODY – THE SOURCE OF ATTACHMENT

D (on seeing Babaji bowing down to a corpse): Babaji, why do we bow down to a corpse?

Babaji: Anybody who can give up this body, under whatever circumstances, deserves to be paid respect to, because attachment to the body is the greatest attachment. To stop identifying with it, even though it may be in death, is a great act.

86. A MONEY MAKING MANTRA

Babaji never wore his spirituality on his sleeves. Often, people came to the *ashram* to simply enjoy the natural surroundings and have a good time. Babaji would welcome them, cook for them and laugh and joke with them. There would never be a trace of disapproval or disdain in his speech or behaviour. At the same time, he always enriched them, even in these casual interactions.

Visitor: Babaji, please give me a *mantra* to make money.

Babaji (laughing): *Arre,* do you think if I had such a *mantra,* I would be sitting here in this simple *ashram!*

Visitor: No seriously Babaji, some people make so much money, why can't I?

Babaji: That depends on your *karmas* and destiny. There is a limit to the kind of money each one can make. But who knows, sometimes, you can also 'outwit' fate.
Visitor: How is that so Babaji?
Babaji : Listen to this folk story that I just read -
A young disciple lived with his master and learnt many vidyas from him. He looked after the master and his family with utmost love and devotion.
One day the master decided to go on a pilgrimage. His wife was in the last few months of pregnancy and so he requested the disciple to ensure a safe delivery of the child in his absence. At the time of delivery, *guruma* was with her female attendants, while the disciple stood outside incase of an emergency. Just then, a young man hastily tried to enter the delivery room. The disciple was livid with anger – 'Who are you and how dare you take the liberty to enter my *guruma's* chamber while she is in labour, without even taking permission?'
The man was stunned, as no one had dared to speak to him in this manner. 'I am *Brahma'*, he said. 'I write the fate of people on their forehead as soon as they are born. This child is about to enter into the world and you must let me in immediately.'
Alright,' said the disciple, 'but only if you promise to tell me what it is, that you will write in this child's fate.'
Brahma said, 'Even I do not know that beforehand. I simply put my pen on the forehead and it gets written.' 'Alright', said the disciple, 'in that case you must tell me what was written, on your way out.' Time was running out and *Brahma* was cornered. Hastily he made the promise and rushed within.
On coming out, the disciple confronted him, asking for the information. Brahma said, 'I will tell you the fate but if you reveal it to anyone, your head will break into a million pieces. The child is a boy with a terrible fate. Poverty will dog his life. A buffalo and a sack of rice is all that he will ever possess'.
The disciple was shattered. What a terrible destiny for the

offspring of a great soul.

Years passed by. Once again, the *guru* wished to go on a pilgrimage, and once again, *guruma* was expecting a baby. Instructing him as before, the master left.

On the day of the child's delivery, once again *Brahma* came. Again, the disciple insisted that he could enter only on the condition that the fate of the child was not kept a secret from him. *Brahma* had no choice but to agree.

On the way out he told the disciple, 'this time over, it is a girl but with a similar fate. She is destined to live the life of utter penury, while prostitution will be her only means of livelihood. And remember, if you reveal this to anyone your head will split into a thousand pieces.'

The disciple was filled with rage, unable to understand the injustice to the progeny of a great master. But *Brahma's* dispassionate declaration left no room for any emotional outburst.

Years passed by. The *guru* also passed away and the disciple roamed the jungles practising his *sadhana* devotedly.

One day, remembering *Brahma's* prophecy, he was siezed with the desire to visit his *guru's* children. He returned to the village of his student days and after much inquiry, found the whereabouts of the 'son'. As prophesied, he lived with his wife and two emaciated, undernourished children, with a buffalo and a sack of rice as the only possessions. 'Verily who can reverse the workings of fate!' he thought. Knocking at the young man's door, he introduced himself. The disciple suggested that if the son, would listen to a plan that he had for him, the son would be able to outwit fate and lead a life of comfort and good fortune.

'And, what is that plan?' asked the young man skeptically.

The disciple said, 'Tomorrow morning, go to the market and sell your buffalo and sack of rice for whatever price is available. From that money, feed the Brahmins of the village with the best of food and let your family also enjoy the same. However, make sure that you save nothing for the morrow.'

Incredulously, the young man stared at the disciple. 'Am I mad to gamble away whatever little I possess', he said. But his wife, who was a woman of faith was somehow attracted to the words of the mendicant disciple and urged her husband to try out the plan. After all, she thought, 'anyway, we do not have much to lose.'

The next morning, the young man executed the plan. Fifty Brahmins from the village were fed and for the first time in their lives, the young man's children had a feast. Fate, they felt, had smiled upon them. The Brahmins left satiated and in good humour, blessing the couple.

Only, the young man's heart was filled with anxiety. Penniless, he worried for the future, almost angry at the mendicant's intriguing plan. He passed the night sleeplessly.

As was his habit, in the morning, he went to the cowshed to feed the buffalo. He saw a buffalo waiting there as usual, while nearby lay a sack of rice. Remembering the prevoius days events he thought, 'poverty even makes me hallucinate. I had sold my buffalo yesterday. So this creature here can only be one of my imagination.'

But the buffalo and sack of rice were for real because *Brahma's* prophecy had to be fulfilled! The young man could not be deprived of what fate had decreed for him. The buffalo and sack of rice thus stood replaced!

The mendicant disciple then took leave of the young man advising him to continue with this plan of selling his buffalo and sack of rice daily and spending the returns to feed Brahmins. 'Remember', he cautioned, 'do not try to save anything for the morrow and you will be saved from penury.'

Then he asked the young man for his sister's whereabouts. Hanging his head in shame, the young man confided that she was a blot on the family name. She had taken to prostitution because of dire poverty and he therefore, had nothing to do with her.

Learning of her whereabouts, the mendicant disciple proceeded in that direction. Once again, he introduced himself and offered a plan of action that would relieve her from her painful existence. 'Tomorrow', he said, 'when a visitor knocks on your door, insist that you will open it only if he carries a bowl full of pearls of the first water. Do this tonight and I will meet you in the morning.'

Desperate to break out of her life of ignominy, the young girl agreed. What did she have to lose after all? she thought.

Many customers came and went that night, sniggering at the pompous demand. It was now only a few hours before dawn. The young girl was dejected at the failure of the plan. But *Brahma's* prophecy had to be fulfilled! She must lead the life of a prostitute and make a living out of that. So, an hour before dawn, *Brahma* himself, in the form of a visitor knocked on her door. He stood with a bowl of pearls in hand, in fulfillment of the condition. The young girl happily welcomed him and thus the night passed.

Overjoyed she conveyed the happy turn of events to the mendicant disciple. 'Good', he said. 'There are very few men who can bring a bowl full of pearls daily and so whoever brought you these pearls last night will have to continue to do so every day. You will now have only this man as your lover and husband.'

With one masterly stroke, the disciple gave his beloved *guru's* daughter the status of a goddess!

'Now', said the mendicant, 'sell these pearls, keeping nothing for yourself. From the money, feed the *Brahmins* of this village and you too enjoy the feast to your hearts content. Every night, this man will visit you with a bowl full of priceless pearls but each day, you must sell them and feed *Brahmins,* saving nothing for yourself. If you follow these instructions you will lead a life of dignity and enjoy good fortune. If, however, giving in to greed, you hoard, then you will sink into your earlier ill-fated days.'

With these instructions, the mendicant left.

He rested for a few days in the shade of a tree and soon decided to carry on with his pilgrimage and *sadhanas*.

On the day of his departure, waking up early to prepare for his journey, he saw a figure in the distance, coming his way. On scrutiny, he saw that it was a beautiful young man who was leading a buffalo and carrying a sack of rice in one hand and a bowl of pearls in the other.

'Who are you? he asked. In disgust, the man threw down his sack of rice and said, 'you wretched, clever fellow! I should have never told you about the fate of those two children. My pen wrote their destinies and thanks to you, in order to fulfill them, I have to carry this sack of rice and buffalo to the young man daily. Then I dress up in all finery and carry this bowl of pearls to the young lady. My head has gone bald carrying this heavy load and my feet hurt with this daily duty.'

Weeping, *Brahma* pleaded, 'when will you relieve me of this terrible fate young man?' The young mendicant said, 'only when you promise them a simple life and happiness.'

Brahma did just that and thus fate was outwitted.

Visitor : OK Babaji, so from tomorrow, I will sell my shop and donate everything to the *ashram*, keeping nothing for myself. Of course I hope that the next morning my shop materialises again or I will have to become a babaji!

Babaji : (laughing uncontrollably) – Let me give you a *Shri Yantra*. If you keep it in such a way that light falls on it, and if you apply a red vermilion spot to it every day, I can assure you that your monetary condition will improve.

87. BHAGAVATI DOES, NOT WE

A disciple was unable to contribute to the *ashram* work, and was feeling guilty about that.

Babaji: Do not worry if you are unable to participate. A time will come when you too will be required to participate. In a cricket team, not all the 11 players come out all at once to bat. They come one by one, when their time comes and when the captain sends them. Your time will come too. When it comes, play fully, and well. Nevertheless, to know when it is time for you to play, you will have to be alert at all times. When it is your turn to play, play and leave the rest to Her.

Until you feel that, 'I have to do'- nothing is going to be 'done'. Until you have an ego that, 'I will do something and show', nothing is going to be done. Only when you work with the *bhava* (attitude or feeling) that,'*Bhagvati* does'- will work be done. Until then, there will be only guilt, stress, and anxiety. In any case, it is She who does, not we. When you play the game of life thus, see the joy and only the joy that permeates your being.

88. RIGHT AND WRONG ACTIONS

D: Babaji, what is this thing about right and wrong action? How does one know?

Babaji: It is what you are that is important. The *Buddha* has said, "*Sahi aadmi galat kaam karega, toh uska natija sahi hoga aur galat aadmi sahi kaam karega toh uska natija galat hoga.*"

If a right (aware) person does a wrong thing, the result will be right. And, if a wrong (unaware) person does a seemingly right thing, the result will be wrong.

89. THE MYSTERIOUS WAYS OF KARMA

A disciple was telling Babaji about her grievances against a person at whose hands she had suffered many injustices -

Babaji: Would you like me to punish her? I can do so with my yogic powers.

D: No Babaji. What is the use? Let bygones be bygones.

Babaji: That's the spirit. I was testing whether sentiments of revenge still lurked in your mind. Always remember, whatever *Bhagavati* does is for the best and whatever happens are the fruits of your own *karma*.

D: So, is it that Bhagavati desired, that I be unjustly humiliated?

Babaji: See, whatever has already happened, can only happen with Her sanction. It is best to live with that attitude. Live in the moment and always be alert and attentive in all your actions.

D: Or, is it that, I must have treated her, or someone else, unfairly and and therefore, I am also a victim of injustice? Is that what you mean by *karma*? Is there an account book up there?

Babaji: Yes. However, the workings of *karma* are not easy to understand. You know the *Bhagvat Gita* says, 'mysterious are the workings of *karma*.' They cannot be understood as a simple addition and subtraction. Anyway, how is knowing all this going to help you? Why do you want to know? You simply apply yourself to your *sadhana* and in due course, you will understand everything. For now, just accept the will of God and pray, 'Let thy will be done'. In this way, slowly you will go beyond the fruits of good and bad *karma*.

90. OUR MINDS MUST BE IN GOD

D: Babaji what should be one's attitude to the world and the work that is at hand?

(Just then a group of ladies who had been working at the *ashram* throughout the day, came to take leave and claim their wages).

Babaji (to the ladies): So, have you completed your allotted tasks?

Worker: No Babaji, but I have to rush. My child is ill. I promise to complete it tomorrow.

Babaji (to the disciple): Life has to be lived. God has sent us here to do some work, and that too, happily. Look at these women, while working, their hearts and minds are in their homes, and at the end of the day, they rush with love to their homes. We too have to do our work, but our hearts and minds have to be in our real home, the centre of our Consciousness. Our minds must be in God. At the same time, there should be no negligence of the work to be done. Do it with full zest, care and skill, yet be anchored within. Your attitude to your life should also be like your attitude to your work. Anchored from within, do what outwardly needs to be done.

The great poet *Rasakhan* has said *"rasakhan Govindahi yaun bhajiyo, jimi nagari ko chit gagari mien."* Worship Govind like the woman whose attention is on the pot of water on her head. Though she is apparently engaged in conversation with her friends, her attention is on the pot of water. Thus, not a drop of water spills out, as she walks along freely and quickly.

91. THE SECRET OF WORK

Visitor: Babaji, I was thinking that I should devote my time to *puja, patha* etc. It is a good way to spend one's life.

Babaji: What are you doing now? Where do you work?

D: Nowhere. I tried many jobs, but a job is not my cup of tea.

Babaji (sternly): You can't do ordinary work and you wish to do God's work. This human birth is a *'karma yoni'*. Here, everything is achieved through work. If you do not work, the *shaktis* within you will become impotent.

'sakal padaratha hai jug mahi, karma hina nara pavata nahi'

All that you desire is there in this world, but men devoid of action cannot attain it.

You lack the energy for ordinary work but you feel you can do *sadhana*! What do you think finding God is all about –an entertainment, a pass time or an adventure? It requires the greatest energy and courage. I suggest you first learn to do a job with dedication, skill and devotion.

D: (after the visitor had left) Babaji, you tell us *'ayasad sakalo duhkhi nainam'*... something like that, meaning, 'all are miserable doing work'. And here this poor man wanted to adopt a life renouncing work, and you sent him back to work. (Laughing) I think *gurus* just like to confuse.

Babaji: Laughing heartily and then in a more serious tone –

आयासात्सकलो दुःखी नैनं जानाति कश्चन ।
अनेनैवोपदेशेन धन्यः प्राप्नोति निर्वृतिम् ॥

All are unhappy because they exert themselves in doing. But nobody knows this. The blessed one attains emancipation through this instruction alone.

Babaji continued: Blessed are they who 'do' nothing.

D: 'Do' nothing? You just sent this poor man away to 'do' something!

Babaji: *Arre laddu,* all exertion is of the ego. Work that is motivated by your lusts and egotistical desires will only result in *duhkha*. The ego likes to achieve, accomplish, get, win... And if it fails in this effort, it is sad, dejected, depressed, discouraged... When working, if you swing between happiness and unhappiness or experience any form of worry, anxiety, doubt, fear, self importance or pride, know that it is your ego working, know that you are attached to the results, know that your motives are not pure or selfless. Such work can only bring *duhkha* or sorrow.

Inwardly you have to be inactive, free of desire, lust for gain or self-interest of any kind. I do not mean material gain alone. The ego is very clever. It can let go of material gain in return for some psychological gain in the form of praise. It is the psychological gain or loss, which you have to renounce. Outwardly, the hands and legs are free to engage in action but the inward state must be free of any desire for gain.

D: And what about this man who did not wish to do any work?

Babaji: That also springs from the ego. It is a desire to not work. It could be due to sloth or fear of failure or laziness to apply his mind. In his case, having to do work gives him *duhkha* and pain. Wherever there is the *duhkha bhava,* there you must look for signs of ego.

D: So that's the spirit in which you want the *ashram* work to be done?

Babaji: Yes. For that, you will have to rise above your petty ego. Only then will you be able to 'do' what 'needs to be done'.

D: Phew Babaji! So now we have to work on the ashram and also on our ego!

Babaji: It is better you work on your ego first.

D: But Babaji, what about *bhaktas* who have given up all work and devoted themselves to *sadhana*?

Babaji: Look at their state of mind. Love of God permeates every cell of their body. The spiritual path is not one of the things they toy with. It is an intense, all consuming love, which leaves no room for anything else, not even sleep and hunger. Then there is destiny also. Some are meant to live in the world and do God's work. Some leave the world. *Bhagavati* decides – leave it to Her. Anyway, only the inner state is important.

92. WORK AT THE ASHRAM

Disciples often lived with Babaji at the *ashram* and were allocated duties during the course of the day, but always with a word of caution.

Babaji: Even work must be done by the *sadhaka* in the right measure. Secondly, the fatigue felt must convert itself into knowledge. Mindless, mechanical work is of no use.

93. WORK JOYFULLY

To disciples working at the *ashram* –

Babaji: Work done joyously, is work well done. What is more, God likes work done with that attitude. Work done with *duhkha bhava,* reluctantly and resentfully, will always be slipshod, half done and untidy. It is an insult to God.

94. HOW DID YOU FARE IN YOUR EXAMS?

Babaji(to a child): So, how did you fare in your exams?
Child: Not too well.
Babaji: Who fared well then?
Child: Some other boys.
Babaji: And pray why?
Has God given them an extra hand or leg?

95. THE REAL CORRECTIVE ACTION

Babaji chided a little boy for some wrong that he had done. Hurt, he started crying.
Babaji: If you cry in helpless self-pity during a calamity, or when chided for your wrong doing, you will lose vital energies and the lesson learnt will be immediately washed away by your tears. The act of crying will automatically replace the real corrective action to be taken.

96. DECIDING IS NEVER A PROBLEM

D: Babaji, I think I have decided on this particular course of action.
Babaji (laughing): Oh yes, go ahead and decide. Deciding is never a problem. The problem starts when one has to put decisions into practice. Most people are happy taking a decision, as if that is itself the action to be taken.

97. WHAT SHOULD BE ONE'S ATTITUDE TO LIFE ?

D: Babaji, what should be one's attitude to work, family, relationships, sex ... ?
Babaji: You remember that *stotra* I had recited for you? It is by the great seer *Bhagvan Shankaracharya*.
आत्मा त्वं गिरिजा मतिः सहचराः प्राणाः शरीरं गृहं
पूजा ते विषयोपभोगरचना निद्रा समाधिस्थितिः ।
संचारः पदयोः प्रदक्षिणविधिः स्तोत्राणि सर्वा गिरो
यद्यत्कर्म करोमि तत्तदखिलं शंभो तवाराधनम् ॥

Oh *Shiva* , You are my very soul and your consort *Girija* is my Intellect, The life forces within (*pranas*) are my siblings and this body my home. The many beautiful things of the world are the instruments of worship and *puja*, And sleep is the state of *samadhi*.
Wherever I go, I am only performing circumambulations to You; whatever I speak is a prayer to You. Whatsoever actions (*karmas*) I perform O *Shiva*, they are worship to You alone.

If you can live your life like this, then all your actions, thoughts and relationships will be pure and blameless.

~

On Spiritual Practices...

Ananda Yoga

What is the use of practices if mind games continue?
What is the need for practices if mind games have come to rest?

What is the use of practices if the play of Bhagavati is
not seen within and all around?
What is the need for practices if only the play of
Bhagavati is seen within and all around?

What is the use of practices if there is not total Awareness?
What is the need for practices if there is total Awareness?

What is the use of means if you have lost sight of the end?
What is the need for means if the end itself becomes the means?

Why all this talk of means and ends when after
all only One exists?
Ananda (joy) is the means; ananda the end,
Ananda alone is all that exists.

~

98. GOD IS A SENSE OF JOY

D: Babaji, I want to find the Truth.[1]

Babaji: Have you ever enjoyed the company of true friends?

D: No.

Babaji: Have you ever been in love?

D: No.

Babaji: Have you enjoyed the sheer beauty of Nature?

D: No.

Babaji: Have you ever enjoyed the fine arts or had a 'passion' in which you have lost yourself completely?

D: No.

Babaji: If you have never experienced any form of joy, how can you find and recognize God and Truth!

99. ON THE MEANING OF LIFE

D: Babaji what is the meaning of this life?

Babaji: '*Shri maata* - She is the meaning and measure of all that there is.'

This is the very first name of *Bhagavati* mentioned in the *Lalitasahasranama.* Only the Consciousness that pervades everything gives meaning to Life. When you have a first hand experience of that Consciousness, then you have found the meaning of life. When you identify only with that aspect of yourself, then you have found the meaning of Life.

When you can see, feel and recognise that Consciouness in all forms of creation and resonate with it all the time, in all situations, then you have found the true meaning of life. All *sadhana* is to attain this state of purity and integration.

100. ME AND MINE

D: Babaji, when will I find God?

Babaji -This 'I', 'me' and 'mine' is the real problem. Until the 'I' exists, there is no God. Let go of the 'I' and its preferences and

1 The 'D' in all conversations refers to Disciple.

prejudices, and God is always there.

101. BEYOND BELIEF AND DISBELIEF

A visitor: Babaji, *main bhagvan ko nahi manta hoon* – I don't believe in God.

Babaji: *Manana, aur na manana ek hi baat hai* – Belief and disbelief are one and the same thing.

Manana, na manana chhod ke, janane ki koshish karo – Setting aside belief and disbelief, try to know (experience) God.

102.SELF-REALISATION IS SIMPLE

Once, on the trip to the Himalayas, we were having a cup of tea at Nilakantha Mahadeva. It was dark outside and the disciples were in a receptive mood.

Babaji: *Ishvar* is in everyone. Rather, as the fish is in water, we all are in *Ishvar*. For the fish, its body, food, drink, house everything is in the water, is the water. The fish may be unaware of it but its complete universe is in and of the water.

Similarly, the *pancha mahabhutas* or the five elements evolve out of each other. The *akasha tattva* is the first and the subtlest evolute from eternal Consciousness, which we call *paramatma* or *deva*. Wind (*vayu*), fire *(agni)*, water *(jala)* and earth (*prithvi*) evolve from ether *(akasha)* by a process of materialisation and manifestation. From the highest to the lowest, all is a transformation and transmutation of that Supreme Consciousness. In the final analysis, all is God.

Therefore, though we may be unaware, everything is *Ishamaya*. However, till 'me' and 'mine' exist, until this petty 'I' exists, you cannot come face to face with God. When 'I' dissolves, you cease to see 'differences', and merge with the One that is above, inside and around you. The important thing is to be aware of this Real form of ours and to live in that Consciousness all the time. *Aur bas ho gayi mukti* - self-realisation is simple!

D: Babaji, you make it all sound so simple.

Babaji: You are the living Goddess (*sakshat Bhagavati*). When will you learn to live in the full glory of your true nature? How long will you go on limiting and constraining yourself? Joy, Peace, Power is all in you. Just live in that Truth and you are free.
D: If it is so simple Babaji, why are we not able to do it? Why this struggle to find that which is closest to me?
Babaji: See, it is like this. It is very easy to mix colour in water. However, it is difficult to separate the colour once it is mixed in the water. Pure Consciousness is like water. The desires in the form of colours mix in it and colour the Consciousness. Then to purify that Consciousness one has to resort to *mantra, japa,* meditation, and other yogic practices.
D: So you agree Babaji, that *mukti* is not all that easy.
Babaji: *Arre,* if a sinner and fool like me can find God, why can't you?

103. 'WHO AM I'?

A disciple had come to Babaji very dejected.
Babaji: Remember, every phase is a passing phase. Good or bad, it will pass. So why don't you draw your mind to that which is permanent? Let us do this small exercise –
What is it that you identify yourself with? Is it your body? Can you call this body your self? Your body was once newborn, and then it grew older, then reached adolescence, then youth and now is middle aged. Soon it will get old and die without leaving a trace. So certainly, there is no permanence in this body. It cannot be the essential you, the Self. The essential 'you' has to be changeless. Tell me that entity which has been continuously in/with you since birth, and has remained unaltered.
Can it be your relationships? For sometime your mother was the center of your existence and to some extent your father. Friends in school and college and friends of the family formed

the outer ring of your relationships. That changed when you married. Husband and children took center stage. That too will change. You have seen many relationships come and go. Whether strong or weak, they all pass away.
D: Babaji, I identify with my mind.
Babaji: And what is it that you call your mind? Feelings, thoughts, habits, preferences, likes, dislikes, stale memories of past experiences, intellectual ideas and ideologies? Have you not seen that all of them are constantly changing? They wax and wane according to the needs of the time and the whims of your ego. Even your talents and intellect can be cultivated or will rust, if you allow them to lie unused. And when you die, they will all die with you.Who are you and what is yours in all this? All this is the realm of *maya.*
D: What is *maya*?
Babaji: *'Ma'* means 'not', *'ya'* means 'that'. 'That which is not', which has no substance because it is constantly changing is *maya.*
D: So who am I, the Self?
Babaji: These are merely things that you have read. Meditate on that query. Do *chintan* and *manana* (deep thinking) on that. The answer is not some bookish information. The answer has to come from you. It has to be an experience, a response of your whole being. Then you have to live your life in the light of that answer.
(Babaji sits in a state of deep meditation chanting away his favourite verse from the *Avadhoota Gita*)

संविद्धि सर्वकरणानि नभोनिभानि
संविद्धि सर्व विषयांश्च नभोनिभांश्च ।
संविद्धि चैकममलं नहि बन्धमुक्तम्
ज्ञानामृतं समरसं गगनोपमोऽहम् ॥

Remember that sense organs are as illusive as the horizon, sense objects are as illusive as the horizon. Remember that I am one, free from impurity, beyond bondage and freedom. I am immortality in knowledge, I am equality in essence, I am like the sky.

104. SHIVABHAVA

D: Babaji, what is Shivahood?

Babaji: See, once *Datta Maharaj* asked *Bhagavati*, "What is the difference between *jiva* and *Shiva*?"

She said-

घृणा लज्जा भयं शङ्का जुगुप्सा चेति पञ्चमी।
कुलं शीलं तथा जातिरष्टौ पाशाः प्रकीर्तिताः।
पाशबद्धो भवेज्जीवः पाशमुक्तः सदाशिवः॥

Hate, doubt, shame, fear and disgust, these five, pride of your family and character and finally all concepts; these are the eight bondages. Bound by these you become a *jiva* (individual contracted consciousness), free of these you are *sadashiva*, always in a state of Shivahood – joyful, free and all-encompassing.

Babaji continued: If you can reach a state where no person, situation or object arouses hate, fear, disgust or shame in you, then you have experienced *shivabhava*. If you can reach a state where the poison of doubt does not touch you, then you have experienced *shivabhava.*

In short, if no life experience triggers a negative reaction in you, then you have experienced *shivabhava.* Similarly, if you are not a victim of either superiority or inferiority complex, then you have attained *shivabhava.* And, when negative reactions and complexes are left behind, then all concepts and judging will fall off. The mind stuff comes to an end. Likes and dislikes, preferences and prejudices will vanish and you are set free. You are *Shiva*. Since *Shiva* is in all things, at all times and in all states, you are bound to experience *shivabhava* sometimes. But, to experience this *shivabhava* at all times, to be *sadashiva*; that is the final goal. The purpose of all *sadhana* is this – to be completely and fully free of all inhibitions and restrictive tendencies once and for all.

D: My god Babaji, what a tall order that is, but what a great state to be in. I really envy the free souls.

Babaji: Never envy the *siddhas.* Befriend them and ask for their grace. Surrender to the *gurus* and the *gurumandala.*

105. THE ONE-EYED ONE RULES

Babaji: The important thing on this path is to open the inner eye, the *ajna chakra.* When you see the grand vision of a life uncoloured by your petty stakes, when you see life as it is, in Nature's plan, then there is no cause for sorrow. That is why our Goddess is called *'Ambika'* – She who is the Vision. That is why we say –*' kana karega raaj* – the one eyed one shall rule.' This one eye is the eye of vision, the third eye. If that is opened, then you can afford to close these two eyes of duality and sleep through life. That eye, can be opened only by the grace of the *guru* and intense *sadhana.*

106. WHO IS READY FOR SADHANA?

D: Babaji, how does one know that one is ready for *sadhana*?

Babaji: Truth is in everyone in a dormant state. But, when the desire to know it arises, then the journey has begun.

D: And, how does the desire arise?

Babaji: The *Bhagavat Gita* says that there are three types of people who desire to know God – the man who wants success/wealth, the miserable man and the seeker of Truth. So you see, even those who have worldly pursuits turn to God; but it is only by the supreme grace of God that one begins to seek Truth.

It is as the *Avadhoota Gita* says -

ईश्वरानुग्रहादेव पुंसामद्वैतवासना ।

महद्भय परित्राणाद्विप्राणामुपजायते ।

It is only by the grace of God that a soul or two long for union with Him and escape grave danger.

When the pleasures of life hold little attraction for you, when you are drawn to the pure life, when the company of holy men delights you, when tears of joy fill your eyes on hearing the name of God and when your *vrittis* (mental modifications) begin to turn inward, then you are ready for *sadhana*.

Qualities like patience, humility, faith, intensity and courage make the soil fertile for the seed of 'the love of God', to grow. You have to water this seed with your *sadhana* and daily practice. Then the seed sprouts in the form of peace, joy, bliss and love.

D: Babaji, before I met you, I would prescribe different disciplines for myself. Does this random *sadhana* have any meaning?

Babaji: Yes, of course. It is because of that *sadhana* that you meet a *guru*. There is a *sadhana* that you do before you meet a *guru*, and then there is a *sadhana* that you do after you meet the *guru* which is prescribed by him. Finally there is a *sadhana* you do after you have attained self-realisation. That is the real *sadhana* when you experience the bliss of ecstatic Love.

107. TIME IS THE REAL CURRENCY

D: Babaji, I have no time for *sadhana*.

Babaji: Time is the real currency. You come into this world with a mind-body complex and some time. You spend time to get money. Be careful how you spend this currency of time.

108. COMMITMENT TO TRUTH

D: Babaji, my worldly duties pull me in one direction and spiritual *sadhana* in another...

Babaji: (laughing) Ah, you know that Urdu couplet –

ना खुदाही मिला ना वसाले सनम, ना इधरके रहे ना उधरके रहे ।

Neither god have I found, nor the joys of the arms of my beloved!

Oh, I am neither here nor there!
(In a more serious tone) There must be an inner commitment and single-minded devotion to Truth even though engaged in worldly activities and duties.

109. NO EVOLUTION SEEMS TO BE TAKING PLACE

D: Babaji, I have seen people spending so much time doing *pujas* and taking God's name, but still no evolution seems to be taking place. Why is that so?

Babaji: Unless there is deep enquiry, introspection, and probing into the layers of one's ego and workings of one's subconscious mind, the doing of *japa* and *pujas* and recitation of God's name is only a waste of time.

110. HERE GOD IS THE ONLY SUPPORT

D: Babaji, my friends and family cannot understand my inward journey.

Babaji: *Beta,* worldly relationships are of use only as long as you are of and for the world. Outside that, in the inward journey, they have no place. There you have to walk alone; the only support being God. Do not look for the support of human beings in this inward journey. The world can only give you selfish love. Love of God is selfless. You know we have a saying that the poet or creative person *(shayar),* the lion *(sher)* and the hero or the seeker of Truth *(suput),* all walk alone.

111. MEANS AND METHODS ARE UNIMPORTANT

Once, during the trip to the Himalayas, the disciples were seated on the banks of the Ganga, late at night –

Babaji: This is a journey into ourselves.

D: You mean an inward journey?

Babaji: Inward, outward; with form, without form; these are all concepts of the mind. In the final analysis, they merge. Sometimes an outward journey leads you inwards, sometimes an inward journey leads you outwards. Truth is one and all pervading. Use whatever means or direction appeals to your sensibilities and is in harmony with your nature. The only important thing is your intention to shed the ego and merge with God. Whatever means and methods are used, intense awareness and genuine search for God are what is important. Means and methods are incidental on this journey.

112. LIFE IS A FLOW

Once, while sitting on the banks of the Ganga, in the Himalayas –

Babaji: We see the water and the leaves and flowers that float upon it, but we do not see the flow, the undercurrents. We are unaware of the unrestricted free flow. Human life is also an unrestricted free flow if only we could go beyond the surface happenings and personality. The personality is like water that is held in a bottle. It is of practical value. But if you mistake that for the Flow, you restrict yourself. Most of the time, we not only feel that we are the bottled water, but we also make sure that the cork is tightly closed! We identify the flow with the bottled water, but its actual essence is the current underneath. Life too, can be truly fathomed with the undercurrent of joy.

Look at that big boulder in the middle of the river, trying to obstruct the flow. However, the flow finds its way – if not this way, then that way, but it moves along. It takes along with it all things that are light. But you cannot flow because of your ponderous ego and are left behind to stagnate.

The small islands that dot the river are to experience the flow. Your pilgrim spots, sacred places and rituals, can be compared to those islands. They take you close to the flow; but they are not the flow.

When the boat is in the river, it internalises the motion / flow, and not the water. Similarly in life, one should internalise the joy and not get stuck in the morass of events. One who is aware of the Joy, can internalise the flow and can experience it from moment to moment. Such a one becomes a *siddha.*

D: Then Babaji, why at all do we bother with these incidentals and externals of temples and *yantras* and rituals?

Babaji: The journey is a whole. The inner and outer all have their place here. They enhance and support each other.

D: Babaji, each time you tell us so many things, but they do not go in our mind – *dimag me jata nahin.*

Babaji: *Arre, dimagwali baat hi nahi hai yeh* – the mind cannot comprehend these things. They are not thoughts. They are levels of Consciousness, beyond thought.

D: Then what should we do?

Babaji: Nothing.

D: Then we will forget them.

Babaji: I have sown a seed, when the time is ripe, it will sprout. Worrying is of no use. I am not giving you some information that you have to cram, remember and worry if it is forgotten.

D: Then what should I do?

Babaji (embracing the disciple)**:** Nothing. Enjoy some *pakodas* (snacks). At least, that is not too difficult to understand, is it!

113. COSMIC ORGANISATION

D: Babaji, on the one hand we say that Truth is One, and on the other hand we have a litany of Gods with detailed descriptions and prescriptions of worship. There are rules, regulations and rituals of how each one of them has to be invoked. Even the colour and type of flowers to be offered to each one of them is fixed. So, how does one reconcile this plurality, with that One All Pervading Consciousness?

Babaji: It is like an organisation; but, of cosmic proportions. Just as the President or Prime Minister ultimately sanctions all decisions, but we have to apply to the proper department, in the prescribed form, and as per the rules and regulations; so also that One Consciousness has to be approached with the right protocol and procedures. However, when, through the power of your *sadhana*, you have direct access to that One Entity, you may drop all procedures.

114. CHID VILAS & CHID SVARUPA

D: Babaji, I can fully accept that Higher Intelligence and Flow, but my rational mind cannot understand elborate rituals, and multiple gods. Why are they necessary?

Babaji: See, it is like this. Just as you have structured organisations for efficient functioning and systematic division of work, so also, religious liturgy and multiple gods are an expression of cosmic organisation. It is from nature alone that we have learnt to organise and create systems. Can we ever create anything without the help of Nature? Can you think of a single invention that man has made independent of Nature? Nature's glorious Play (*leela*) guides us and teaches us always. This cosmic organisation is *Bhagavati's chid vilasa,* her playful manifestation. But behind this interplay is *chidsvarupa* or undivided, unconditioned Consciousness. That is akin to the Flow. However, both *chidvilasa* and *chidsvarupa* are God. Wherever our faith rests, there itself, in that very form, the whole truth will be revealed to us. Do you see the compassion of Nature?

115. READING IS NOT SADHANA

Babaji was reading the *Ramayana* and telling some interesting stories to a disciple.

D: Babaji, can I take this book to read?

Babaji: No. Just do the *sadhana* that I have asked you to do.

D: But is this also not doing a *sadhana*?

Babaji: No. Reading cannot substitute the *sadhana* given by the *guru.* Can recipe books substitute cooking? Books may keep you in the company of Truth but to become Truth, you will have to do *sadhana.*

116. THERE IS NO NEED TO READ BIG RELIGIOUS BOOKS

A disciple had attended a discourse in which the topic of *Rajayoga* was discussed. Fired by the talk, she came home and pulled out the *Bhagvad Gita* and *Jnaneshvari* from her private library, to brush up her understanding of some spiritual concepts. Babaji happened to come home that very day.

Babaji: There is no need to read these big *granthas*. Just remember God. God is inside you, outside you, and in every particle. Serve this God and don't ever feel proud of your devotion. That is all you need to do.

117. SPIRITUALITY HAS TO BE LIVED

D: Babaji, can you explain to me the difference between *advaita* and *samkhya*?

Babaji: And what will you do with all that information? Spirituality does not lie in collecting information on philosophies or techniques of spiritual discipline. It is a living fount. Truth has to be lived from moment to moment, here and now, in full awareness.

See, because you are my disciple, I am telling you this very bluntly and frankly. Otherwise, if intellectuals come to the *ashram* to pick my brains, I simply bring out a mixture of honey and water, which resembles whisky and sit there sipping it! (Laughing) All their intellectual curiosity takes a back seat and their moralistic inhibitions surface.Throughly disgusted, they leave me alone!

118. IS KNOWLEDGE OF SANSKRIT ESSENTIAL ?

D: Babaji, I am handicapped. I do not understand the *granthas* because they are in Sanskrit.

Babaji: So? What does that have to do with self-evolution? *Panditya* or scholarship is not essential for self-realization. Was *Mirabai* a Sanskrit scholar, were *Ravidas* or *Kabir* scholars and Sanskrit *pandits*? Enlightenment has nothing to do with material or intellectual endowments.

119. LEARN TO SIT STILL IN PADMASANA

D: Babaji, I don't seem to be making any progress in my *sadhana.*

Babaji: A *sadhaka* should never get discouraged in the practice of his *sadhana.* Never allow this form of negativity to enter you. It could also mean, that you are doing the *sadhana* with expectation of some reward of a 'spiritual experience'. That is not *sadhana*, that is *baniyagiri* (trading, profit making mentality). You know, the great saint *Rabia* used to say, "O God, if I pray from fear of hell or greed of heaven, then please do not answer my prayers."

D: OK, I understand Babaji. But please tell me what is it, which is coming in the way of my progress?

Babaji: First of all, you must learn to sit still in *padmasana.* Without that, it is not possible to reach higher states. Why don't you practice this as an exercise – whatever you do, whether it is reading, cutting vegetables or even while talking to someone, just practice sitting in *padmasana.*

D: OK. Babaji did you also practice *asanas?*

Babaji: *Arre,* when *Gurumaharaj* locked me up in that cave, I used to practice *asanas* for long hours to keep my body lithe and agile in that limited cave space.

120. THE POWER OF AUM

As Babaji lived with the idea of the *ashram gurukul* and thought deeply on it, he was convinced that the only way to create a fearless and creative generation of youngsters; would be, through the practice of *'aumkara'.*

Babaji: These academic studies are not very difficult. It is just that the levels of energy and consciousness of the students is low, because they do not practice any form of spiritual

discipline. These children must be taught *pranava sadhana.*
D: And what is that Babaji?
Babaji: *'Pranan unnayate iti pranava* – that which raises the life force to the higher centers of Consciousness, is *pranava.'*
D: I do not quite understand this concept Babaji.
Babaji: Whatever is energised, is energised by the life force or *prana*. But generally, the life force is spent in fulfilling the lower desires and lusts.Thus it is locked and trapped in the lower centers of Consciousness situated on the spine.When it is thus trapped, we work in an uncreative state. Therefore, you have to free the life force from these lower centers and make it rise through the higher centers, to reach the brain.
D: So how will *'aumkara sadhana'* help?
Babaji: In two ways. Firstly, scattered energies will be gathered and that itself will be energising.Modern life is stressed, fragmented and out of tune with Nature. Energies are thus dissipated and disintegrated within us. The recitation of *'aum'* will primarily file these energies in order. It will bring about inner orderliness in a person.
Secondly, as the life force is gathered and raised, the energies will actually increase.
This *'aumkara'* has the power to make man commune with God. The whole of Nature vibrates and resonates to the sound of this *mantra*. Such is its power. Can you imagine with what ease children practising it, will be able to tackle academic studies!
D: And how is it to be recited?
Babaji: The three syllables, *'A', 'U'* and *'M'* have to be individually recited and awakened in different centres of the spine.
Visualising the form of *'aum'* in his body, the *sadhaka* has to, while reciting and elongating the syllable *'A'* trace this first *matra* or digit of *aum* by taking his Consciousness from the navel center *(manipur chakra)* to the lower most

center(*muladhara chakra*) at the perineum.

Then climbing up along the spine, at the heart center, the syllable *'U'* has to be recited. Again, elongating the sound of this syllable *'U'*, Consciousness has to be raised along the spine tracing the second *matra* of this *mantra.*

Finally, the *'M'* sound has to be recited at the center of the head and brought down to the tip of the nose reciting this final *matra* of the *mantra.*

When the sacred syllable *'AUM'* is recited in this way, electro-magnetic energy fields will be created within the *sadhaka* that will unleash his hidden energies and potentials. A practitioner of *aumkara sadhana* will have boundless energy and a grip of the subtle essences of things. He will get deep insights into whatever subject he chooses to study. The recitation of *'aumkara'* will also sharpen the discriminative powers of his mind. Thus he will even be able to rise above useless desires, plans and projects with the practice of this *sadhana*.Thus, *'aumkara sadhana'* will not only create fresh energies in you but will also help preserve them. Both these processes are important for creative thinking and living.

D: I have still not completely understood what you are trying to say Babaji.

Babaji: You just start practicing it and watch the effects of its vibrations within you. Real understanding is not intellectual understanding but actual experience.

121. PRANA IS EVERYTHING

D: Babaji, I do not understand this concept of *prana.*

Babaji: Then what is the use? You have not understood the essence! Life force and *pranic* vibration is everything. That is why *Bhagavati* is called *Praneshvari.* If you tune into the *pranic* vibrations of anything, you can resonate with it and communicate with it. In addition, if you can raise your *pranic* life force to the higher centers, then you can shift the dimension of your existence.

D: Babaji, I still do not understand!

Babaji: Forget it. Anyway, these are practical experiential things and beyond a point, theoretical understanding is of no use. Thousands of books have been written on the subject; but what is the use? Continue doing your *sadhana* and someday you will have the experience. Then, the words of the teacher and the explanations in books, will have meaning.

122. THE IMPORTANCE OF CHANTING

D: Babaji, I enjoy chanting *bhajanas* and *kirtanas.*

Babaji: Why?

D: Because the mind becomes *'leena'* or dissolved in that.

Babaji: Why?

D: I don't know.

Babaji: Rhythmic chanting balances and harmonizes the *'pranas'* or breath. It is for this reason that chanting gives peace and a sense of well-being. People are not even aware why chanting is enjoyable. But you know, the biggest enemy is the mind. It can make anything mechanical. Never do anything mechanically or habitually. This habit-forming tendency is the enemy of man. Mechanical singing of *bhajanas* and recitation of *mantras* is of no use. People do *sadhana* mechanically and then complain that it is not bearing any fruit. *Sadhana* must be attentive while being regular and continuous – there is just that subtle line. Finally, you must live the Truth exhorted in the *bhajans* that you are singing.

123. THE VARKARI SAMPRADAYA AND SINGING OF HYMNS

D: Babaji, tell us something about the *varkari sampradaya* and the singing of hymns penned by great saint poets. It is believed that, simply by singing these hymns, one can attain the Supreme.

Babaji: Those were great saint poets, great *siddhas,* who in their compassion, created these hymns for the middling *sadhaka,* who is not yet ready, for higher *yoga sadhana.*
D: And what is the meaning of the word *'parayana'*? Why should one do *parayana* or reading of the *Bhagvata* or *Ramayana* etc?
Babaji: *Parayana* indicates *prayana* or to go towards that, to undertake that journey. They are signboards. If, a milestone says – 'Pandharpur – this way', then, to reach Pandharpur, you have to move in the direction indicated on the signboard. However, if you start walking towards Poona, then obviously you will never reach Pandharpur. People do the *Jnaneshvari parayana* and mouth spiritual jargon, but behave in a manner completely opposed to that. How can they ever hope to reach the final destination? Rituals, *japa,* reading of sacred texts etc., if done without understanding, or without living the Truth, are of no use. Such practices can even cause harm and result in smug oratory and hypocritical behaviour.

124. THE REAL MEANING OF RAMA

Babaji, lost in meditation in the early hours of morning, was chanting –
'sri ram, jai ram, jai jai ram; sri ram, jai ram, jai jai ram.'
When Babaji, in his deep voice, intoxicated with the love of God, would recite even a simple chant like this, disciples would feel a deep peace and quietude descend into their hearts. Simple prayers would become potent with meaning.
Babaji (opening his eyes)**:** We should understand what is the significance of *'rama'* in our life. It is no use just muttering *'laddu, laddu'* (sweets, sweets). Unless you taste the sweets, you cannot enjoy them. All that may happen is that, by saying *'laddu, laddu'*, some day you may feel – let me try this *'laddu'*. Similarly, by chanting *rama, rama,* you may some day feel the real urge to be with *rama.*

Rama, Vitthala, all are inside you. *Rama* is the *chaitanya* in you.*'Ramyate iti rama'* – that Consciousness, which is charming and delightful in you, is *Rama*. *Sita* is the *buddhi* or intellect and *Ravana* is your ego. *Ravana* does not allow *Rama* and *Sita* to unite. The impure mind is *Ravana's Lanka*. The body is *Ayodhya*. *Ayodhya* can never be conquered. It means that none can escape death and disease.

But, what is most important, is *ravana dahana* or the burning of *Ravana;* which is symbolic of conquering the ego. To rise above 'I' and 'mine' is the final goal of spirituality. It takes millions and millions of years to evaporate the ego. It poisons everything it comes in touch with. If you put, even one drop of poison, in a pot full of pure milk; it is enough to make the whole pot impure. So is one trace of ego, enough to nullify all good deeds and *sadhana*. Whatever good deed is done, feeds the fire of your ego, if you have not conquered it. You may even feel proud of your devotion and the *sadhana* that you do. What is the use! Can real devotion exist where there is pride? Can you conquer delusion and sorrow if there is pride? Can you rise above duality, when this source of all duality exists? To conquer the ego is the greatest and only *sadhana*. *Ravana* has to be killed, to establish *Rama rajya* or the sovereignity of peace and beauty.

125. YOU SHOULD BE DRUNK WITH RAM NAMA

Babaji: This spiritual journey should consume you with madness and leave no room for anything else. You should be drunk with *'rama nama'*. This state is also recognized as a state of Supreme Love.

Once, the emperor *Akbar* was saying his prayers. A *dasi* who was rushing to meet her beloved, unwittingly kicked the emperor who was in a prayerful state.

Irritated, the emperor asked, "Can't you see that I am praying?"

The *dasi* said, "My lord, drunk in the love of my mortal

beloved, I did not even see you, as I rushed to meet him. I am surprised oh great emperor, that in spite of being engaged, in that act of divine love (prayer), you still were conscious of the outer world and the little discrepancy in my behaviour!"

Babaji continued: That is why, one of the names of the Goddess is, '*madhvipanalasamatta* – languid with drinking wine'. This wine, is the wine of joy that comes from tasting Truth, from being drunk with that Divine Love.

126. THE MEANING OF EKADASHI

D: Babaji, I cannot take food today, I am observing *ekadashi.*

Babaji: Can you tell me what *ekadashi* means?

D: Fasting.

Babaji: The five sense organs, the five organs of action, and the mind; when all these eleven *(ekadasha)* are in your command, when you have mastered them, then you can do *ekadashi.* Fasting is then, the natural outcome of that state of your mind. Fasting has to 'happen', it is a reflection of that state of mind. If the body practices abstinence, while the mind feasts on objects of the senses, what is the use? All rituals point to an inner state, try to grasp these. If by eating *sabudana khichdi* (a preparation eaten while fasting), God can be attained then by now many would have realised God.

D: So do you ever fast, Babaji?

Babaji: Only on *Mahashivratri.*

127. HOW MANY TIMES MUST I REPEAT THIS MANTRA ?

D: Babaji, how many times must I repeat this *mantra?*

Babaji: Listen to this story –

A saint used to meticulously count the number of times he repeated the Name. One day, he overheard a conversation between a milkmaid and her friend that changed his approach to *sadhana.*

The friend asked the milkmaid, if she was keeping an account of the milk that she was gifting to her beloved everyday. Laughing, the maid replied, "I have no clue – all I know is that, I love him. In love, there is no counting."
The saint let go of his rosary that very moment. If this poor milkmaid, does not keep count, of the milk she gifts her beloved - a mere mortal; how can I calculate or count this act of Divine Love!
Babaji continued: Besides, you must understand, that every time you say the 'Name', you may not be saying it with full awareness. Such chanting of the Name is of no use. So, are you going to count the number of times the beads are turned, or the number of times they are turned in an integrated state of Consciousness? So why bother with all these difficult mathematical exercises. Let *Bhagavati* do the counting.

128. THE MEANING OF BHAKTI

D: Babaji, I like *bhakti yoga.*
Babaji: O my god, these big words scare me. Can you tell me what is meant by *bhakta?*
The disciple is unable to answer.
Babaji: *Bhakta* is one, who is never *vibhakta* or separated from the Lord. A *bhakta* is one who is bathed in the light and love of God at all times. When you are thus united with God, you can be said to be practicing *bhakti yoga*. Mere chanting and singing and sentimental devotion is not *bhakti.*

129. DO SADHANA WITH UNDERSTANDING

Babaji (to a disciple)**:** So, do you understand the meaning of the sacrificial ritual *(havan)* that you seem to perform everyday at your house? What is the meaning of this offering of sesame seeds *(til)*, rice *(tandul)*, and clarified butter *(tup)* in the fire?
D: I do not know. It is a family tradition, so I continue doing it!
Babaji: Then, what is the use? These three respectively stand

for lust *(kama)*, anger *(krodha)* and greed *(lobha)*. You have to burn these up; and that is the real sacrifice. If this awareness and understanding is not there, you will perform these rituals all your life and yet, achieve nothing.

130. WHY RECITE THE LALITASAHASRANAMA?

D: Babaji, tell us how and why the *Lalitasahasranama* should be recited?

Babaji: These names of the Goddess are forms and names of your very own Consciousness. They are descriptions, or facets, of your own enlightened state. These states have to be actualized in your own being. You have to live them.

D: How can mere recitation and repitition produce an enlightened state?

Babaji: You are right, it cannot. Only if you recite these Names, in a thought-free and attentive state, will the benefit accrue.

D: How is that so?

Babaji: Anything done with attentive awareness, gives rise to a state of total integration. The greater the attentiveness, the deeper is the integration.

When you are thus integrated; thought, speech, action and the state of Consciousness become one, and the names of the Goddess that you recite become your own form and nature.

Have you noticed, how devotees even begin to look like their *ishta devatas* or chosen personal Gods? Awareness has this power to integrate and actualise.

While reciting the verses, sit in *padmasana* and perform the *jnana mudra* (i.e. thumb and forefinger are joined and the other fingers extended) with the right hand and the *dana mudra* or *varada mudra* (i.e. all the fingers are stretched and held together, pointing downwards in a gesture of giving), with the left hand.

These are also names of *Devi*. She is referred to as *Jnana mudra,*

Varadaa and *Padmasana* in the *Lalitasahasranama*. So you see, the *Sahasranama* also contains guidance on how you have to say it.

Assuming these *mudras,* sit in *asana* and recite the *Lalitasahasranama patha* with total awareness. If you do so, the Goddess is easily pleased.

131. THE TEMPLE IS IN MY HEART

D: Babaji, where are the temples of *Lalitadevi* in India?

Babaji: Ah, many people have asked me that question. Many are the temples of *Lalitadevi.* I will take you to them when we go to the Himalayas. But I feel the real temple is in my heart. Actually, it has just struck me that the *Lalita Sahasranama* does mention where the temple of *Devi* is. It says, '*antaramukhasamaradhya, bahirmukhasudurlabha* – She can only be worshipped within you, outside you, she is difficult to find.' So there, I was right in my understanding!

132. CONTRADICTORY NAMES OF THE GODDESS

D: Babaji, there are many contradictory names of the Goddess in the *Sahasranama.* At one time she is referred to as *'bhogini'* or 'the Enjoyer', and in another place she is referred to as '*yogini'* or 'One who is free of mental modifications'. In another instance, She is referred to as the one who fulfills desires – *'kamadayini'* and '*kama'* or 'desire'; while at other times, She is '*niraga'* and *'ragamathana'* or 'Remover of desires.' All this is very confusing Babaji.

Babaji: *Kama* is a *shakti,* a Force, a Power, like a mighty river; and *raga* is like the many small rivulets that fragment the mighty river. *Raga* dissipates that Energy through attachment and incessant, innumerable desires, weakening that great force of the Will. Therefore, She destroys *raga* or attachment, so that energies are available for higher states. However, *Kamashakti* is the basis of life and therefore She bestows it.

In the *sadhaka,* this very *Kamashakti* is converted into higher energies. Again, *yogini* and *bhogini* are not contradictory. You can 'enjoy' only when desires and mental modifications cease; until then, you are only 'being enjoyed' by your cravings and desires.

D: What do you mean when you say, 'being enjoyed by cravings?'

Babaji - You are their slave. Only a master *(yogini)* can be an enjoyer *(bhogini).*

D: But, how do I know for sure that I am enjoying as a master and not as a slave? After all, the mind is very clever and deceitful.

Babaji: Yes, that is true. You have to become sensitive to the slightest flicker of greed and lust within you. Truth is very subtle. To understand it, you need a subtle vision. All grossness must go. Remember the name of *Devi* – *'bisatantutaniyasi,* as fine as the fibres of a lotus stalk.' Your understanding must become fine, like the fibres of a lotus stalk. *Sadhana* is meant to fine tune this sensitivity and give rise to ruthless honesty with oneself. (Smiling) Until then, to be brutally honest with the disciple, is also the role of the guru.

133. LIVING TRUTH

D: Babaji, what is the importance of spending time with the masters and knowers of Truth?

Babaji: There is a transmission, a rubbing off that happens. One candle lights another. Because the master is free from all limiting and constrictive tendencies, because his Consciousness is centred, these very qualities gradually rub off on the disciple. My *Gurumaharaj* used to say – 'I am that touchstone, which makes a touchstone of everyone that I come into contact with.'

Remember those names of *Bhagavati* –

नीरागा रागमथनी निर्मदा मदनाशिनी ॥
निश्चिन्ता निरहंकारा निर्मोहा मोहनाशिनी ।
निर्ममा ममताहन्त्री निष्पापा पापनाशिनी ॥
निष्क्रोधा क्रोधशमनी निर्लोभा लोभनाशिनी ।
निःसंशया संशयघ्नी निर्भवा भवनाशिनी ॥
निर्विकल्पा निराबाधा निर्भेदा भेदनाशिनी ।

She (i.e the Knower of Truth) is free of strutting pride; hence She destroys the pride of those who come in touch with Her. She is free of anxiety, ego, greed, and delusion, hence She removes the greed and delusion of those She comes in touch with.
She has no sense of attachment and 'mineness';
hence She destroys the same in others.
She is sinless and destroys sin.
She is free of anger and quenches the anger of those
who come in touch with her.
She is free of doubt and destroys the doubt of others.
For her the 'becoming' process has ended; hence She puts
an end to your becoming process.
She is free of thought constructs and unobstructed,
She is devoid of all divisiveness and destroys all divisiveness...

All knowers of Truth i.e Masters, are Her very form and serve the same function. It is in this sense that the company of the learned, knowers of Truth helps.
See, it is like the story of a little boy, whose mother brings him to a *guru,* because he has the bad habit of eating jaggery all the time.
The *guru* listens to the problem, and asks the mother to bring the child again, in the following week.
The next time, when the boy comes, the *guru* gently tells him – "My dear, don't eat so much jaggery. It is not good for you."
The mother is perplexed and asks the *guru,* why he needed one week to give this simple advice, to the young boy? The guru

smiled and said, "Because till last week, I myself loved eating jaggery!"

Babaji continued: It is only what you are, that can rub off on others.

134. THE PANCHA MAKARAS OF TANTRA

D: Babaji, what are these *pancha makaras* of *Tantra?* Are they relevant today?

Babaji: Those rites should not be taken literally. The five *'makaras'* are symbolic.

Madira stands for the intoxication caused by the arrogant ego. Drink that up. ***Mamsa*** stands for the gross sense of 'mineness.' ***Matsya*** stands for *matsara* or hatred and jealousy. Eat that up. ***Mudra*** stands for joy. *'mudam dravayate iti mudra* – that which gives joy is *mudra.'* ***Maithuna*** stands for the end of all duality. Known and unknown, good & bad, light & dark, *dnyan & adnyan*; these are all *dwaitas*. All *dwaitas* or dualities should become one ultimately.

The actual ritual does involve sexual practices and the use of intoxicants, but these are for the evolved *sadhaka.* The ritual is based on the principle that in a state of pure and heightened *shringara* (eroticism), God realisation was possible. Do you remember the name of *Bhagavati* – *'shringararasasampurna* – She is the Erotic Love'? Actually, in states of heightened love, sorrow and fear, a state of *samadhi* can be achieved. People think that these are short cuts, but to qualify for their use, the practitioner has to be highly evolved and sensitive and adept at intricate psycho-physical yogic processes. Only when the *shiva bhava* is potent in the *sadhaka,* and not before his Consciousness had ascended to the higher *chakras,* could he practice these *sadhanas.* And then too, only under the supervision of the *guru.* The highest purity is required for these *sadhanas.* Do not understand this simply as mating out of lust.Not a trace of ego must remain, if you have to practice these *sadhanas.*

The slightest impurity in the *sadhaka* will reverse the entire process of evolution. Even in case of the sexual act, it is what you 'are', that is important. Your actions can be evolved, only if you are pure and evolved. As such, this *path* is fraught with danger. I think it is better to call them intense modes of *sadhana* than abbreviated modes or short cuts. On this path there are no short cuts.People assume, presume and imagine that they are ready for these *sadhanas.* They simply satisfy their lust giving it a holy name. Thus our *shastras* have been defiled and abused. These *sadhanas* are not to be trifled with by anyone and everyone.

D: What is the symbolic significance of *maithuna*?

Babaji: One should understand the deeper meaning of sexuality and not take it literally. On the physical, psychological and spiritual level, the sex act should be understood as the coming together of *Shiva* and *Shakti*. The partners should see *Shiva* and *Shakti* in each other. Only then will the act culminate in good progeny. A sexual act without this awareness is nothing but lust.

Just as in a marriage, the blood of the two partners becomes one, only if the union culminates in progeny, so also the *Shiva* and *Shakti* principle in you should unite and give birth to Bliss. *Shakti* resides in the lowest center, at the base of the spine, in the centre of Consciousness called *muladhara chakra* and *Shiva* resides at the top of the head, in the highest center of Consciousness – the *sahasrara padma.* The energy at the base of the spine, has to be raised to reach the top of the crown. In mythology, this is symbolically expressed as the marriage of *Shiva* and *Shakti.* This is *Shivratri* – the night of *Shiva,* the night of His union with his *Shakti.*

135. THE IMPORTANCE OF DEEP THINKING

D: Babaji, is cogitation or *chintana* of higher truth of any importance or is it just of dry intellectual and academic significance?

Babaji: No. Sincere, deep pondering, inquiry and contemplation of the Truth, produces heat (*tapa*) so to say, sublimates energies and raises subtle energies in you as if by a process of conversion.

136. WHY SHOULD ONE MEDITATE?

D: Babaji, why should one meditate?

Babaji: *Gurumaharaj* used to say, 'Wash the plate and keep it, after it is used.' So, when will you wash the plate?

D: After you have eaten something in it.

Babaji: The pleasurable and painful experiences of the world are the food that your psyche eats. You have to clean the *chitta* of their residue that is in the form of psychological memory. You have to clean the plate, irrespective of whether you have eaten a dish of your liking, or otherwise. Moreover, what would happen if you did not clean the plate?

D: It would collect fungus and emit bad odour.

Babaji: What if you were to still neglect washing it?

D: The fungus would convert into maggots.

Babaji: And, if you further procrastinate in cleaning it, what would happen? The maggots would eat up the very plate and you would have to get a new one. Similarly, a stage may come when layers of impurity would have gathered on the pure *chitta* and the psyche is beyond repair. Life is short and alas, you would have to put off the cleaning for the next birth. Many such births have passed in procrastination. Why don't you wake up now!

137. SOME DOS AND DON'TS IN MEDITATION

Babaji: From tomorrow, when you sit for meditation, wash your face, hands (upto the elbows) and feet.

D: Please tell me some other dos and don'ts of meditation Babaji.

Babaji: Don't see these as rigid 'dos' and 'don'ts'. That will produce stress. These are devices to get into that state. They are tools for awareness building, a kind of psychological preparation. People take them as rigid rules and then get bugged up or feel guilty and lose the most important thing – awareness.

There is a great psychological advantage in doing the *sadhana* at the same time, in the same place and with the same *samagri* or tools like lamp, incense, the seat (*asana*) etc.

Meditating at the same time, activates the inner clock. The *sandhi kalas* (sunrise and sunset), the *brahma muhurata* (3 a.m.) and the time around midnight are good for meditation. But then again, it is better to meditate at any time, than to not meditate at all. This is an act of love. If *Bhagavati* sees intense love then she forgives all transgression of rules. Meditating at the same place, creates the right vibrations, that intensify as you do *sadhana*. The paraphernalia puts you in the right mood. Ideally, you should sit in *padmasana,* but if you cannot, then take a pillow and sit on it in such a way, that the knee points touch the floor. Put the right palm over the left one and let the thumbs touch each other. This is to close the body circuit, so that energies are not dissipated. The spine must be erect to allow the energies to rise. Then sit still with eyes closed.

First, visualise the *guru* in between the eyebrow center and then visualise your personal God in the heart center. Fugitive thoughts will come and go. Let them. All you have to do is watch them. Do not prohibit or encourage them and do not identify with them.

Apply the same process to your breath. Watch it come and go, without regulating or restricting it. Be with the breath. Then, when in a quiescent state, you may chant the *mantra* silently or better still, watch it being chanted inside you, by *Bhagavati.* While meditating, if the mouth is filled with saliva, drink that. It is *amrita,* the life giving nectar. If there is any perspiration while meditating, rub it into the body.

Group meditation can also be beneficial because, if one person goes deep into himself, there is a collective rising of energies, touching all by that inner quietude.

D: Is that why, when we sit with you, there is greater stillness and peace? In fact Babaji, I enjoy just watching you meditate.

Babaji (laughing)**:** Why ? Is this a performance or something? Initially it is ok, but eventually you will have to cook your own *khichdi!* At the moment you are in the courtship period of this love affair, but ultimately you will have to marry, right?

D: Babaji, how shall I become more disciplined.

Babaji: It is not a state of becoming. There has to be inner discipline.

D: What is that ?

Babaji: There has to be sincerity, only then will the discipline happen.

D: And what is sincerity?

Babaji: To begin with, it is an honest intention. Eventually, it is a state of integration of your mind, body, speech and emotion. As a result of this, your intentions, thoughts and actions will completely match. The real indiscipline is this lack of integration. You say one thing, you feel another, your thoughts are running after a third thing, while you do something that is altogether different. How can there be discipline? But don't worry, with *sadhana* everything will fall into place. Just do the *sadhana* with love for God and She will take care of everything. You have to do the *sadhana* with love and not with force.

D (self-indulgently)**:** But I tend to become lazy.

Babaji: *Pitai hogi pitai* – you need to be thrashed. I will have to use *Gurumaharaj's* methods. Self-indulgence and sentimentality are not to be tolerated on this path!

138. A MEDITATION TECHNIQUE

D: Babaji, how should I meditate?

Babaji: Meditation is a happening in which the knower, the known and the act of knowing become one. Techniques are all incomplete to reach that state of mind. It is a happening, which is the culmination of *yoga sadhana* and all inner purificatory processes. It marks the cessation of all thoughts.

To begin with, let me teach you a simple technique to still the mind. With *Bhagavati's* grace, over a period of time, the meditation may happen.First, remember and visualise the *guru* in the *ajna chakra* or the centre between the eyebrows. Then, remember and visualise your *ishta devata* or personal god in the heart centre. The *guru's dhyana* is to be done from head to foot because the mind must finally rest at the feet of the *guru*. In addition, the *dhyana* of your *ishta devata* must be done from the foot to the head of the diety.

Then, take deep and slow breaths to still the mind. As the mind becomes still, thoughts will lessen. Between the center of the brows you will see a darkness. Gaze upon that emptiness intensely and relentlessly. With *abhyasa* or dedicated application, you will see there, at the centre, a flame of light. Be with that as long as you can.

One hour of meditation is superior to *puja* and *archana* done for a whole year.

139. A TIBETAN WAY OF MEDITATION

D: Babaji, are there any quick ways of getting into the meditative state, especially when one is pressed for time in the busy urban schedules?

Babaji: There is a Tibetan way of meditating –

First, visualise the *gurumukha* (*guru's* visage) in your heart centre. Then, visualise a flame in the *guru's ajna chakra*, which is in the centre of the brows. Then, slowly see and experience the expansion of that flame to envelope everything, including yourself. Remain in that state as long as you can.

140. MEDITATION NOT FOR EVERYONE

Reading about some meditation courses –

Babaji: I find it difficult to understand how meditation courses are conducted here, there and everywhere, for any one and everyone. Meditation is not for everyone. If for example, a person is very depressed, sitting in meditation will be downright harmful for him. Sitting in silence, with only his own negative thoughts for company, can only unhinge a person and drive him crazy. First of all, it is essential to sort out the issues of one's life and make peace with one's self, before one can sit in meditation. Otherwise, this so called meditation, is also a kind of escape from taking the practical decisions of life.

141. MEDITATION IS TO LIVE IN THE MOMENT

D: Babaji, when I sit to practice *dhyana*, my mind is constantly worrying about what is to be done in the kitchen. What should I do?

Babaji: Go ahead and finish the work in the kitchen. To meditate means to live in the moment.

142. A SIMPLE SADHANA

A disciple was genuinely disturbed because familial duties left very little time for her own *sadhana*. In sincerity, she asked Babaji what was the way out for her.

Babaji: You do this simple *sadhana* – when you are applying *kumkum* (vermillion) to *Bhagavati*, tell yourself, 'this is my very own Self that I am invoking.' When you cook for the kids say, 'this is for *Bhagavati* that I am cooking.' If you are eating, say to yourself '*Bhagavati* is eating.'

When this one *rasa* (mood) of *Bhagavati bhava* permeates everything that you do, when you see Her in every act and person and emotion and when you also see yourself as nothing but Her, your *sadhana* will be done. (The disciple looked at

Babaji confused, not quite understanding or believing that the Truth could be that simple.)

Babaji: This is not just a matter of belief or sentiment, it is a fact. *Bhagvati* is all that there is. Know this for sure. This unbroken *Bhagavati bhava,* itself is self-realisation.

143. HOW TO LIVE IN SAMSARA

Babaji: So, how is your *sadhana* going on?

D: *Arre* Babaji, we are *samsari* people. We have other chores to do.

Babaji: This body itself is *samsara.* So long as you have a body, *prapancha* (mundane acts of survival and maintenance of the body) is going to be there. Does not a *sadhu* need food, clothes and shelter? He also has to survive. But the trick is to live in *samsara,* and yet not to let the *samsara* live in you.

144. COMMITMENT TO SADHANA

Babaji: So how is your *sadhana* going on?

D: I have suffered certain setbacks, so I am not in the right emotional frame of mind for doing *sadhana.*

Babaji: Nothing should be more important to a *sadhaka* than his *sadhana.* The world may come and go, it should be of no concern to you.

145. A SENSE OF URGENCY IN SADHANA

Babaji: So *beta,* tell me how is the *sadhana* going?

D (listlessly)**:** *bus chal rahi hai* – it's going on.

Babaji: You see, when doing *sadhana,* there must be an intensity and urgency, as if life is ebbing away.

D: What do you mean by intensity Babaji?

Babaji: See, in doing your mundane chores and in material pursuits, your attitude should be liesurely, as if the whole of life is spread before you to complete them. Whereas, in the matter of *sadhana,* your attitude should be one of immediacy, as if death is close at hand and this is your last opportunity to worship. This urgency is a mark of your intensity.

146. A SADHAKA'S FRAME OF MIND

Babaji: So how is your *sadhana* getting along?
D: Good. But I am very depressed.
Babaji: Then what is the use? *Sadhana* must be done in a state of complete good cheer or it is of no use.

147. THIS IS WRONG UNDERSTANDING

Babaji: So are you doing your *sadhana*?
D: You told us, '*aish karo*' - live joyfully. Therefore, I do not get very tense about my *sadhana*. I am now at peace. After all, you are there to take care of everything, right?
Babaji: This is what I call wrong understanding.Until you make a commitment to dispel the darkness of the ego within you and prepare to walk fearlessly on the path, even if a crore of *Krishna's avataras* take birth, it will be of no use to you. Beware of false peace; it is laziness masquerading as peace and surrender. Know it as one more trick of your mind.

148. CONTINUITY IN SADHANA

D: Babaji, what if I cannot do *sadhana* everyday?
Babaji: Continuity in *sadhana* is very important. However, it is possible that, on some days the pressures of your worldly duties may take precedence. That is Ok. What is not Ok, for example, is that at the time of sadhana, you sit and watch TV, or engage in useless conversations and other such meaningless activities.

149. GRADUALNESS IN SADHANA

A disciple was forcing himself to sit for long hours in meditation.
Babaji: If you cook the *khichdi* too much, it will get burnt.

Sadhana should be done naturally and should deepen gradually.

150. SADHANA IS ATTENTIVENESS

Babaji: One who remains attentive in whatever he does, is a *sadhaka.*

151. ON 'BECOMING' A YOGI

A disciple who was a serious *sadhaka* was getting worked up and highly attached to her very *sadhana.* She wanted to quickly, 'become' a *yogi.*

D: Babaji, when will you teach me that technique of meditation?

Babaji: I don't know. I am in the mood to eat some *pakodas!*

D: Ok. In that case, I think I will just sit and meditate.

Babaji (laughing)**:** All right, you go ahead and strive to be a *yogini* while I enjoy my plate of *pakodas* (snacks)!

152. THE WHOLE OF LIFE MUST BECOME A SADHANA

D: Babaji, because of worldly duties, I am not able to find the time for *paramartha* or the highest goal of life. What shall I do?

Babaji: The spiritual path is of ease, bliss, and joy. Is that not what you are also looking for in your day-to-day life? For a *sadhaka,* these borderlines must blur and merge and the whole of life must become a *sadhana.*

153. WHATEVER A GURU ASKS YOU TO DO, IS A SADHANA

D: Babaji, when will you teach me some *sadhana?*

Babaji: And what have I been doing so far? Whatever a *guru* asks you to do, is a *sadhana* – even if it be as trivial as, instructions on how to place your shoes, when you enter the house.

D: O, I thought only *mantras* and techniques of breathing and meditation can be called *sadhanas.*
Babaji: When will you allow the distinctions between life and *sadhana* to drop?

154. DEALING WITH PAIN

D: Babaji, how does one deal with the pain and sorrows of life? Is Nature just testing us through them?
Babaji: Whatever is, is the fruits of your own *karma*. Take it cheerfully. Some people choose to do difficult *sadhanas;* others are 'made to do' difficult *sadhanas* by Nature, in the form of life experiences and situations. Treat the sorrows and painful experiences of life as the difficult *sadhanas* that Nature is making you do.
D: I did not understand Babaji.
Babaji: See, for example, some people may choose to stand the whole day while doing *mantra japa* or other such *sadhana.* Now that is a discipline they have chosen, so they feel proud and have a sense of accomplishment on doing it. However, if on some day, you have to stand for hours because the bus does not come, take that as a *sadhana* ordained by Nature. Accept it without grumbling and complaining. If for some reason, you cannot get food the whole day or cannot find the time to eat, take it as Nature wanting you to do *upavasa* or fasting! If you learn to surrender to the lows of life, great devotion and humility will come to you. If physical or mental stress comes your way, say 'Oh, this has been sent to me by my dear *Gurumaharaj'* and the stress and pain will become a *tapa*. By complaining, you lose this golden opportunity to convert a crisis into *tapa.*

155. THOSE WHO NEVER GO TO SCHOOL HAVE NO EXAMS TO GIVE

D: Babaji, why do calamities befall a *sadhaka*? After all, he is walking on the path of truth and so things should be easier, and not more difficult for them?

Babaji: If you join a school, you will have to give an exam. Those who never go to school, have no exams to give. Besides, these calamities are in a sense, a precipitation of the *sadhaka's karma* or past actions, so that he can be free of them as soon as possible. All the calamities that befall a disciple, are in fact due to the blessings of the *guru*. It is also *Bhagavati's* way of weeding out those, who take to *sadhana* to get the goodies of life.

156. ALL WILL EVOLVE

D: Babaji, a person I know, has had no setbacks in life. Is it possible to evolve under such circumstances?

Babaji: All will evolve. This is Nature's plan. Even a stone that lies in a corner, is polished over a period of time.

157. A SADHAKA CANNOT BE OBSTRUCTED

D: Babaji, when I want to come to the *ashram*, many obstacles crop up, but when dealt with, they slowly and miraculously dissolve.

Babaji: '*Sarvanulanghyashasana*', that is one of the names of our Goddess. She overcomes all obstacles, especially on the path of the seeker of Truth. No obstacle can come in Her way.

158. THE AGONY AND ECSTACY OF SADHANA

D: Babaji, on this spiritual path too, there is so much longing and pain and suffering, almost as much as there is on the worldly path.

Babaji: Yes, a famous *shayar* (poet) has said, *'ghame ishq gar na hota ghame rojgar hota.'* When he was asked, 'Why do you want this state of Love that brings you so much pain, striving and sadness?' He replied, 'The human lot is one of pain. If there were not the pain of Love, there would be the pain of sheer survival, getting, and spending. I much prefer the pain of this *ashiqui* or Love in which there is ecstacy.'

159. WORK FOR THE SELF

Babaji, to a disciple who was very helpful in organizational work and fund raising activity for the *ashram* -

Babaji: Why were you absent from the meditation session today?

D: (Mumbles some excuse.)

Babaji: This one will do many things for the organization, but nothing for his Self ! What is the use?

160. IS THERE NO WAY OF GETTING ENLIGHTENED QUICKLY?

D: Babaji, is there no way of getting enlightened quickly?

Babaji: This impatience is the real undoing. Without patience and humility, nothing is achieved on this path.

Let me tell you a story. -

Once, the sage *Narada* was walking along, testing the patience of *sadhakas*. As he walked in the jungle, a *sadhaka* asked him, 'O great sage, when will I be enlightened?' Sage *Narada* said, 'O, you will be enlightened in a couple of births.' 'O my god', said the *sadhaka,* 'that long!' Dejected, he put aside his rosary. Going a little further, Narada met another *sadhaka* who asked him the same question. *Narada* replied, 'O, you will take a few more years to attain.' Depressed, he folded his *asana* and prepared to leave.

Further along the way, he met another *sadhaka* who once again shared the same concern. *Narada* told him, 'See that tamarind tree yonder. To find Truth, you will require as many births as the number of leaves on that tree.' The *sadhaka* looked at him in joyful wonder and said, 'you mean, I will someday be blessed with the vision of God!' And so saying, he started dancing in ecstacy. That very instant he was enlightened!

Babaji continued: You see this patience is a form of humility. If you think that you deserve to be enlightened, you do not. If you can wait in patient humility, then alone Truth can be yours. Remember what the poet Milton has said, "They also serve who only stand and wait." In addition, patience is Love. A lover should be content to just love, without any greed or expectation.

D (laughing)**:** Babaji, you know that famous graffiti – God give me patience but hurry up!

Babaji (laughing loudly)**:** So, you want to eat the *laddus* of enlightenment! You want to have the 'pleasure' of enlightenment! If you desire to be at any place (or time) other than where you are now, enlightenment cannot be yours. Supreme patience means supreme contentment. That is why our Goddess is called '*sadatushta* – always contented.'

D: I will try to be patient but still Babaji, are there no quick ways!

Babaji (on a more serious note)**:** Well, if you want to shorten the time, then you have to heighten the intensity. You know, even reciting the *Lalitasahasranama* just once, can enlighten you. Recite it single-mindedly, with total awareness and identification with the meaning of each name, taking care that no fugitive thoughts impinge on this *ekagrata.*

161. THE DEMONS WITHIN

D: Babaji, who is this demon *Bhandasura*?

Babaji: There are many demons mentioned in our *shastras.* Actually, they are the demons within you. The war is within; and the peace too, has to be made within.

Bhandasura is the demon of sloth, inertia, gross thinking and living. This demon does not allow you to do *sadhana* and discipline yourself. He makes you fall asleep when you are trying to sit in meditation. He covers your mind with grossness, so that you are unable to grasp the higher Truth. He does not allow you to live the spiritual principles that you have understood intellectually.

Then there is *Mahishasura*. He is the demon of lust and ego. He fills you with strutting pride and makes you crave. *Mahishasura* is clever and assumes many charming, chimerical, quicksilver forms. He even masquerades as many virtuous and nice qualities. This is the demon of your ego. Like *Mahishasura,* this ego too is very deceptive, cunning and hard to vanquish. Even the great Goddess Durga, took nine full days and nights *(navaratri),* before She could vanquish him and that too with the support of the divine energies of all the Gods !

One more demon inhabits your body. His name is *Vishukra.* When *Bhandasura* and *Mahishasura* house in your body, you become *Vishukra* or devoid of lustre (*shukra). Sadhana* has to be done to kill these demonic forces within you.

162. WHAT A STRUGGLE SADHANA BECOMES!

D: Babaji, we want to do *sadhana,* but sometimes we are overcome by sleep, sometimes there is no inclination, at other times, issues related to personal life distracts us. Often we procrastinate for no reason at all. What a struggle *sadhana* becomes!

Babaji: What else do you expect when you are fragmented from within.The real culprit is lack of integration and lethargy. The lethargic, *samsari* mind resists change and especially spiritual progress. This is the demon *Bhandasura* in you- the demon of lethargy. There are some *upayas* or remedies for this. When the feeling of procrastination grips you, the feeling that 'I will meditate later', overcomes you, know that lethargy is at work. When you are seized by drowsiness while meditating and yet cannot sleep, know that *Bhandasura* reigns.

To overcome gross lethargy in the form of sleep, eat in moderation and practice *yogasanas.* To overcome subtle lethargy, practice breathing exercises. To overcome laziness, you can also undertake selfless works and eschew useless thinking, fantasising and living in your imagination. Once in a way, try to get up in the middle of the night and practice meditation. At such times, the sense organs are not restless due to fewer distractions and gross sensory stimulations. Keep on striving to reach God until life and breath is there. If in the pursuit of Truth, you have to give up this very body, do not hesitate.When the head and heart will integrate, you will find God. Then life itself will be a *sadhana.*

163. SLEEP AND SLOTH

D: Babaji, my real problem is sleep. I cannot overcome sleep and tend to sleep a lot. Even while trying to meditate, I feel sleepy. What should I do?

Babaji: If you feel sleepy while meditating, roll your head in a circle a few times and the sleepiness will lessen.

In actuality, even when you have slept for 7-8 hours, the real, deep sleep is only for 4-5 minutes and it is that which rejuvenates. But, to reach that state of deep restfulness and to come out of it, takes time. If you master the technique of shortening the process of going into, and coming out of sleep, your actual sleeping time will be incredibly short - as short as 4-5 minutes! It is similar to the act of collecting pearls from the seabed. The time taken to actually collect the pearls is very short. What is time consuming, is the process of reaching the seabed and emerging back to the surface.

However, the problem of sleep has deeper implications.The real problem is that of slothfulness. A slothful mind and body is unaware, whether awake or asleep. Why, even dreams are not remembered clearly. With such sloth, the state of sleep is always present. Even when you are awake, you are asleep! This sloth, apathy and indolence are the demon *Bhandasura* that *Bhagavati* vanquishes. They are the greatest enemies of a *sadhaka.*

On the other hand, if you can retain conscious awareness even while asleep,you will experience the highest meditative state. The opportunity to awaken is ever present in life.

164. MODERATION IN FOOD IS VERY ESSENTIAL FOR A SADHAKA

D: Babaji, what about hunger?

Babaji: Moderation in food is very essential for a *sadhaka*. Extra food is converted into sloth, which is akin to death for a *sadhaka*. At a time, do not eat more than one and a half *chapatis*. If very hungry or over worked, you can eat about two and a half *chapatis*. Never overeat at night, for that will hamper your morning *sadhana*. If you give too much water to a tree, it loses colour, rots and dies. Overfed bodies meet with the same fate.

165. ESCHEW WORLDLY TALK

D: Babaji, my neighbour's sister's friend is too much! She borrowed my neighbour's jewellery and then...

Babaji: Why discuss these things? A *sadhaka* has to avoid petty, mundane and worldly talk. Ignore these issues, especially when they do not concern you at all. Worldly gossip is best avoided. The last thing you should do, is to discuss these matters with a *guru*. You come here to understand a higher life and not wallow in a lower one.

166. WATCHING TV

To a young visitor, spontaneously –

Babaji: Why do you watch so much TV? It will make your mind impure and dissipate energy. How are we concerned with the lives of those fictitious characters? A *sadhaka* especially, must stay away from cinema and TV. Better to immerse yourself in deep thinking (*manana*), pondering upon the higher truths (*chintana*) and reading of sacred literature (*vachan*).

167. WHAT IS WRONG WITH A LITTLE BIT OF EXTROVERSION?

D: But Babaji, what is wrong with a little bit of extroversion?

Babaji: Who is to decide what is little and what is more? If you fall in the company of shallow, extroverted people or read books written by worldly people, describing worldly tales and travails, you will lose the love of God. Their very vibrations will impede love for God. Stay away from them. If you must love, love God, love the messengers of God (the saints), and the words of God as expressed in the religious texts. That way Love will increase in your heart.

168. THE GAP BETWEEN DESIRES

D: Babaji, we know that to desire is to court trouble. But it cannot be denied that, fulfillment of a desire does bring at least a momentary satisfaction.

Babaji: It is not so much the fulfillment of a desire as the absence of it, that gives joy. Between one desire and another, there is a gap. In this gap, due to an absence of desire, the mind is in a quiescent state. The joy and satisfaction comes from this and not from the fulfillment of a desire.

169. I AM A DOCTOR

D: Babaji, won't my home look beautiful if I buy new curtains and adorn it with some potted plants and...

Babaji: O yes, you can do all that and much more, but remember – a *sadhaka* should not expend more energy than necessary, in these mundane concerns.

D: Babaji, on the one hand you say that everything is *Bhagavati,* and all acts should be looked upon as sacred; and on the other hand you chide me for looking after my household. Just the other day you pulled me up for neglecting my responsibility towards my family and today you say just the reverse. I am confused!

Babaji: Try to have right understanding. I guide according to your frame of mind. If I see you losing balance, I pull you in the opposite direction. My advice changes from time to time and person to person. I am like a doctor. I give medicine according to the need of the moment. If you do not have right understanding, you will be confused.

Similarly, when I am addressing a group of disciples, you should know which counsel is meant for you. Spiritual concepts can be comprehended with right understanding alone. Partial understanding, wrong understanding, sentimental or subjective understanding (i.e in a personal context) will never lead to the understanding of the whole Truth.

170. INTERNALISE TEACHINGS

D: Babaji, let me write down what you are saying.

Babaji: Write it in the tableau of your heart.

171. BABAJI, YOU AND YOUR CONTRADICTORY TEACHINGS !

D: Babaji, breakfast is ready. Would you like to take a quick bath before it is served?

Babaji: This *dhyana* (meditation) itself is *snana* (bath). After I have meditated, I feel completely cleansed from within and do not feel the need for a bath.

D: O, good, good! I am also feeling very lazy to take a bath.

Babaji: You had better go for a bath. Bathing is important. It kills the subtle microbes and imperceptible impurities that have collected on the surface of your skin. Until you perfect meditation, you cannot take the liberties that I do.

D (laughing)**:** Phew! Babaji, you and your contradictory teachings!

Babaji laughs.

172. SPIRITUAL EXPERIENCES

A disciple had a deep spiritual experience in the past and was smug in the warmth of that memory.

Babaji: How can he move ahead now? He is still eating the *laddoos* of that experience. All spiritual experiences, however powerful and impressive, have to be left behind if the *sadhaka* has to progress in the pursuit of Truth. These experiences are to help you gauge your journey and strengthen faith; they are simply milestones in your *sadhana.* In a journey, you cannot afford to clutch a milestone to your heart, or mistake the milestone for the destination.

173. AN EXPERIENCE OF GAJAMUKHA

A disciple once mentioned the experience of seeing *Gajanana* or *Ganapati* when sitting for meditation.

D: Babaji, what is the meaning of that vision?

Babaji: When your senses are turned outward you see the world i.e. *'jaga'.* When they are inverted and you begin to see inward, you will see *Gaja,* the elephant headed God.

174. NOT THAT

A disciple was describing some spiritual experiences she had to Babaji –

Babaji: Whatever experiences you may have, firstly, do not gloat over them or discuss them with anyone. Moreover, whatever experience you may have, remember, it is not That. Experiences come and go, and that which comes and goes is not the Truth.

175. DON'T RUN AFTER SIDDHIS

Once, an interesting discussion was going on and Babaji was sharing insights on Truth with the disciples. Suddenly turning to a disciple –

Babaji: Please get me a glass of water.

D: Babaji, at such times I wish I had a *siddhi* whereby I could continue sitting here and listening to you, while the water would come on its own!

Babaji(laughing)**:** *Arre,* do not run after *siddhis.* They are the greatest traps on this path. They give you a sense of power, increase the ego and there is always a danger of their indiscriminate use. Once during my *sadhana* period, while traveling in the jungles, I met a *Baba* who taught me *mohini vidya.*

D: What is that Babaji?

Babaji: Some *mantras* that can attract and enslave a person to the practitioner.

D (laughing)**:** O, what great fun!

Babaji (guffawing)**:** Ha, listen to the great fun. I tried it on a young girl and she started following me, and refused to leave me, in spite of my entreaties and explanations. She followed me for three days, until in desperation, I fled at night while she was asleep.

D: Babaji, can you tell us something more about this *mohini vidya*?

Babaji: It consists of *mantras* that can cause death, destruction, enslavement and intense attraction in the person on whom it is practiced.

D: How interesting Babaji! Just for the heck of it, can we not learn it?

Babaji: No. I have taught you the means of acquiring the greatest *siddhi*- that of experiencing the Truth and overcoming delusion. It is the mother of all *siddhis* - '*siddha mata*'. Do you remember that name of *Bhagavati*? On this path as in the world, do not run after the temporary and flashy things. Go for the essence. Go for the real Power- my beloved *Bhagvati Shakti.*

176. BEWARE OF SMUGNESS

D: Babaji, now I feel very contented and at peace.

Babaji: Be sure that it is not just complacency. Complacency and smugness kills awareness.

177. PARTIAL REALISATION

D: Babaji, I feel I have at least realized a little bit.

Babaji (guffawing)**:** There is no such thing. Either you are realized or you are not. It has no shades, no partial states. It is whole, always.

178. BABAJI, MAY BE I AM ALREADY REALISED!

D (joking)**:** Babaji, may be I am already realised but don't know it! What are the signs that I should look out for?

Babaji (laughing loudly)**:** You are a funny woman! That state cannot be hidden from others or yourself. It is self-evident. Can a fully pregnant woman conceal her state?

When an unbroken feeling of Oneness engulfs you, when you live and act in the knowledge that only 'I' exist and there are no others, when Bliss engulfs you and you see *Brahman* everywhere; know that you have found God. When you are established in the feeling that, this world and its happenings are a dream and you are simply watching it, and when you live in that awareness; know that you are realised. All the *sadhana* that you do must transform into this living experience. So do you think you are a realised soul?

D: Almost!

Babaji (laughing loudly)**:** Can you be almost pregnant?

179. TRUTH IS NOT SOMETHING TO BE FASCINATED WITH

D: Babaji, I am fascinated by the spiritual path.

Babaji: Oh my god, this fascination is a very dangerous thing. Truth is not something you should be fascinated with. Fascination is a shallow sentiment. You cannot hope to reach the grand truth with it. It is better you do not walk on this path, if that is your motivation.

D: Then what should the motivation be?

Babaji: Intense longing to find Truth at the cost of all else. You know what that requires? A large heart, a huge receptivity! Come with a heart that is this big (spreading his arms). Do you know what that means? Supreme courage.When you go to a *guru*, go with a big and empty vessel.You will have to empty your vessel (mind). Can you empty yourself off all your concepts, preferences and prejudices, your strutting pride in your handful of achievements and intellectual knowledge? Can you stand naked before yourself? That will require supreme courage. This awakening is a rebirth. Are you prepared to die while living? Then alone you can be reborn. In order to see the Reality, can you die to your past, to all that you have clutched as dear to your self, your wealth, name, fame, and relationships? This awakening is a conscious death. Can you consciously, joyously, rush to meet your death? If you have that kind of courage come here, otherwise do not dare to!

180. REALISATION IS NOT A ONCE AND FOR ALL THING

Often times, Babaji would come as if expressedly to share something, as if he knew what was bothering us. He would say what had to be said, and leave. On one such occasion –

Babaji: You know, whatever action happens to be done through you – good or bad – never feel, 'O my god, what have I done!' Face it squarely and say 'So what?'

D: Babaji, I suppose once one is realised, one views one's actions differently. Is that so?

Babaji: *Arre laddu*, it is not that. Realization is not a once and for all thing. It is a dynamic state of vigilance all the time. You may lose awareness - so what? Be aware again. I cannot understand why, even sages like *Vishvamitra,* get complexes and feel that they have 'fallen', when attracted to an *apsara.* So what, get up and start walking again! This self-realisation is a state of constant watchfulness, like walking on a razor's edge. You cannot afford to look here and there, in the past or the future. This watchfulness is important, not your silly, petty, 'right' and 'wrong' actions.

181. ONLY AWARENESS MATTERS

Visitor: Babaji, I can sit watching the mountains and the rising and setting sun for days together.

Babaji: So what is so great about that? Even a cow can do that. What is important in anything that you do, is the level of attentiveness and awareness.

182. RENOUNCE WHAT?

D: So Babaji, how should one practice renunciation?

Babaji: Renounce what? What is yours, that you can boast of renouncing it? The only thing that is yours, that you can take pride in having carefully cultivated, is your ego. Therefore, the only thing that you need to renounce is the ego.

183. WHAT IS THE MEANING OF SANYASA?

D: Babaji, what is the meaning of *sanyasa?*

Babaji: *Sanyasa* means to keep things in their proper place. To never lose a sense of proportion and discretion is *sanyasa.* It reflects an integration of the personality wherein speech, thoughts and acts match and you do what needs to be done, at the right time and place, in the right measure. A *sanyasi* is never out of rhythm. *Sanyasa* is a state of perfection.

184. WHAT IS SIN ?

D: Babaji, the other day someone commented that it is a sin for a married lady to travel alone with you, and for you too, to travel with a lady. Is it so?

Babaji: There is no sin except lack of awareness.

D: And what is this awareness that you constantly ask us to perfect?

Babaji: A vigilant, choiceless, non-reactive attentiveness to every wave of sensual, emotional, mental and psychological movement in oneself, in the light of which life becomes intelligent and conscious. To be the seer and not the seen.

That awareness is what you are. In the final analysis, the goal of *sadhana* is a constant awareness of that Awareness.

185. PRACTICE MAKES YOU PERFECT

Babaji (to an artist disciple)**:** I do not see you practicing your art at all these days. An artist must constantly work on his art, creating new forms and expressions. There should be no complacency. Complacency and smugness is the downfall of any *sadhana.* It turns the talent and *vidya* in you into poison. Hence the saying, *'anabhyase visham vidya* – when untutored and unpractised, a *vidya* turns toxic or poisonous.'

D: I do not understand Babaji. How is that so?

Babaji: Undigested and unpracticed knowledge is like undigested food. It is bound to convert into poisonous toxins. Just as the body does not know how to process half cooked and half digested food, so also the mind does not know what to do with half-baked knowledge. Undigested food either gets thrown out of the body or stagnates and becomes toxic. So is the case with undigested knowledge; either you forget it or there is the danger of haphazard and faulty practice.

Again, the purpose of all knowledge is to remove ignorance and destroy the ego. This ego is the greatest toxin. Only when the *vidya* is digested and fully assimilated, does the ego dissolve into knowledge.Only when the food is chewed and digested does it fully enter the blood stream to nourish and energise. By *abhyasa* or intelligent and intense practice alone, can the elixir of *vidya* or true learning be churned.

186. THIS 'FORGETTING' IS ALSO THE EGO OPERATING

Babaji: Oops, I forgot to bring cow's urine for that person. You know, we forgive ourselves easily if we forget, thinking that it is a minor human slip. However, this forgetting is also the ego operating.

D: How?

Babaji: Forgetting is a form of laziness and all laziness is the ego in operation. Secondly, you never forget things that are important to you. Therefore, it is a form of selfishness, which is also the ego.

D: My god Babaji, I am so forgetful.

Babaji: Now don't get bugged. Ponder deeply and dispassionately over these things without being bogged down by guilt and self-criticism. Because we are lazy and unwilling to ponder, we fall into the guilt mode and put an end to the matter there.

187. THE CASE OF THE WAGON AND THE BRAKES

Once, Babaji came up to two disciples who were living at the *ashram* and spontaneously analyzed what was blocking their progress.

Babaji: This 'X' fellow has the railway wagon (faith or *shraddha)* but no brakes (self-discipline). This 'Y' fellow, he has the brakes (self-discipline) but no wagon (faith) to ride.

188. QUALITIES THAT A SADHAKA MUST POSSES

Once a disciple had gone visiting an elderly lady with Babaji. While leaving, she bowed down to the lady. Babaji was pleased with this act of humility.

Babaji: Humility is a very important quality in a *sadhaka.*

D: Babaji, what are the qualities that a *sadhaka* needs to walk on this path?

Babaji: Many. But importantly, you need **HUMILITY** or an absence of the ego.

नतानां जनानां समस्तां प्रदात्रीम् ।

To those whose heads are bowed down in humility, She bestows everything.

Listen to this story –

Once *Narada* asked *Mahavishnu,* 'Who is the devotee

dearest to you?' *Mahavishnu* referred to a simple farmer, who remembered God through humble acts of devotion that punctuated his life of hard toil. 'What!' said *Narada*, 'greater than me?' *Mahavishnu* then asked Narada to go around the three worlds, carrying a pot of oil on his head. 'Make sure', he further directed, 'that not a single drop of oil is spilt on the way'. Having successfully completed the *pradakshina* (circumambulation), Narada presented himself before the Lord with great pride. *Mahavishnu* asked, 'So, how often did you remember Me on this *pradakshina?*' *Narada* said, 'O, not even once! You see I was too engrossed in the task.'

Babaji continued: To lead a life of prayer, is far more difficult than intricate *sadhanas*. The egotistical, exhibitionist mind, lacking in humility, likes to make a show of commitment and seeks gratification in impressive *sadhanas*. Do not be impressed by complex practices because outer paraphernalia is inconsequential; only the inner state matters. Simple disciplines practiced with utmost devotion, can go a long way. Never feel that a practice which your *guru* has given you, is silly or too small for your stature. Have you heard of *Dandavat Swami*? His *guru* had given him only one *sadhana* – to bow down to everyone, man or beast, whomsoever he met in his day-to-day life. Although laughed at, he obeyed the instructions of his *guru* and lo! simply by doing this, he got self-realisation (*atmasakshatkara*)!

Self-importance is the anti-thesis of humility. A *sadhaka* must guard against that. Have no feelings of superiority and do not expect preferential treatment from man or God. Moreover, Truth is a gift from the *gurus*, never demand it arrogantly nor pompously imagine that you deserve it. No human effort can be commensurate with the glory of God.

This humility is not an outer mannerism. Do not understand these high principles and values as the niceties of social behaviour and put on politeness. You cannot pretend it. Your ego will reveal itself through your smallest acts and words. Neither is it a servile, spineless, lack of courage and self esteem. *Gurumaharaj* used to say, 'Every man must be aware that he has the potential to become God, but must also remember that after all, he is only human.'

Then there is **PATIENCE.**

You can say that it is another form of humility. With it comes forbearance and an unconditional acceptance of life. *Sadhana* too should be unconditional and without expectation or greed for quick results. Patience is also a sign of inner stillness. In stillness alone can the subtle Truth enter you.

D: Babaji, why are we restless?

Babaji: All restlessness is of the ego with its plans and projects, preferences, prejudices, hopes, fears and expectations and a discontentment with whatever and wherever one is. Patience is a sign of the absence of the ego. In your *sadhana,* every time you get impatient that you are not attaining, ask yourself, *'tum kya bade miyan ki dum ho, ki tumhe bhagvan milne chahiye* – are you the esteemed tail of God himself that He should be with you?'

FORTITUDE/COURAGE (*dhairya*) is another 'essential'. Thus, the Goddess is called *'dhira'*. This courage again makes you impervious to the vicissitudes of life and helps you pursue the *sadhana* single-mindedly. With courage comes *vairagya* or non-attachment. Otherwise, *Bhagavati's maya* will make you go weak in the knees.

Have the courage to accept the fruits of your *karma*. You get what you deserve. You must be able to say 'So what?' no matter what life dishes out to you. Life situations are the fruit of your own *karma. 'Tum apne hi khate me se kha rahe ho* – you are only using (eating) from your own *karmic* account.' You and you alone are responsible for your life.

Have the courage to stand naked before yourself, to see the

workings of your petty ego without a need to justify. If you do not accept a sickness, how will you cure it? This supreme honesty in a *sadhaka,* is a form of courage. And to be completely fearless, is to be completely free.

Courage also lies in not being discouraged or demoralised. After much *sadhana,* if the Truth eludes you, know that you still need to purify the *chitta.* In *Bhagavati's* domain, there is no injustice. Continue with the *sadhana* until the end of your life, with increasing intensity and selfless love. With this *dhairya* or patient courage, you will also get *dharana* or a capacity to hold the Truth.

There is also *shraddha* or **FAITH.**

All *sadhana* is grounded in faith. In its absence, it would be anchorless, aimless and a complete waste of time. It would be as futile as preparing to go to a place that you do not believe exists. Faith is a deep, inner sense of Truth that inspires and goads you on the path. It takes care of the poison of doubt that nullifies all *sadhana.* Have faith in the words of the *guru,* the scriptures and trust your own inner 'pull' towards the path. That is why our Goddess is called '*nihsamshaya* – One without a doubt' and '*samshayaghni* – One who destroys doubt.' Faith begets faith. Therefore nurture whatever faith you have, protect it from the poison of doubt and it will increase.

D: But Babaji, what about the pitfalls of blind faith?

Babaji: How can faith be blind? Can awareness be unconscious? Can nectar contain poison? Can darkness exist when there is light? Faith is a light, a form of awareness; it is a deep sense of Truth. It is a yardstick of the purity in you. Blind faith or faith that wavers, is only a trick of your mind and ego. It is based on assumptions made by your ego, when it takes a fancy to something or someone. When something or someone provides a 'shelter' to your timid mind or holds some promise of pleasure, you cling to it. This clinging you call faith. When your assumptions are invalidated, or the object of your faith comes in the way of your self-interest, you lose faith. If your faith is shattered or short-lived, know that it never was faith. Infact, faith brings an end to seeking shelter and clinging. Faith is not in any person or image or any form. In faith, the only shelter is God, that eternal, supreme principle of Truth.

You also need **SINCERITY** or an integration of the inner and outer so that you can live the truth that you understand. Sincerity alone will help you convert understanding into practice. Otherwise, you will only be a facile and glib talker. *Tamas,* inertia or laziness (*pramada*) does not allow you to progress, even after you have understood the Truth intellectually. Laziness or *pramada* in following the teachings of the *guru,* is one of the biggest obstruction to sincerity in *sadhana.* The greatest laziness is experienced in doing the inner *sadhanas* and living the spiritual principles. In fact, the only hurdle on this path is the ego, and the laziness to fight it. A lazy person can never be sincere.

CONTINUOUS DISCIPLINE (*abhyasa*) is invaluable for a *sadhaka.* The Goddess is called '*abhyasatishayajnata* – She can only be known through intense and continuous study and practice.' Discipline both inner and outer is important.

D: Babaji, what is inner discipline?

Babaji: That which is found in Nature, where things are ordered and appropriate, and 'happen', without stress and struggle, at the right time, in right measure.

D: O, how beautiful Babaji, how does one cultivate that.

Babaji (laughing)**:** You cannot cultivate it, because it is not a quality or decoration of the personality. It is a state of being. When all cravings, inner noise, reactions and resistance ends, there is inner discipline. All outer discipline is to support inner discipline.

D: How is that so?

Babaji: All outer discipline is a conscious effort to do what needs to be done, setting aside preferences, predjudices, laziness and the tendency to run after pleasure. In short, it is a conscious effort to set aside the ego. However, when the ego is truly silenced, you will have natural, inner discipline where all painful effort ceases. When you have complete inner discipline, *sadhana* will happen. Until then, follow a gentle outer discipline. Aggressive and forced outer discipline will be self-defeating and divide you with guilt and anxiety. Whatever qualities you try to acquire on this path, make sure that there is no divisiveness in you.

You must have a **SUBTLE INTELLIGENCE** or **SENSITIVITY**. Subtle intelligence is the *sat-asat viveka buddhi*. It is the power of discrimination without which, you will never be able to distinguish the Truth from illusion. Truth is subtle - *bisatantutaniyasi*, remember that name of *Bhagavati*? This subtle sensitivity is the opposite of sentimentality.
D: What is the difference Babaji?
Babaji: A sensitive mind sees things as they are and a sentimental mind sees things as they suit and affect his personal self- interest.
The cultivation of these qualities requires deep, inner *sadhanas* through *manana* and *chintana* of the Truth and, an alert vigilance over the workings of your mind. A *sadhaka* needs these qualities and *sadhana* gives these qualities. They are the means and the end. As you pray intently and intensely, your patience, humility, courage and faith will grow until you reach the final goal when you 'are' all these.
With these qualities, Love of God will manifest in your heart. *Arre,* don't mistake this Love for the love you experience in your youthful days. (Laughing) That love is like firecrackers - attractive and shortlived. (Lovingly stroking the disciple's head) When you feel that deep and divine love for everyone,

then let that feeling flower in your heart. Do not feel proud of it and go around tomtomming it, understood!
Kissan jo bhi pakata hai, sab bech nahi deta. Kuch agalesalke beej ke liye bachake rakhata hai. Usi tarah sadhana mei payee hui cheeje bata nahi dete – The farmer does not sell all that he has produced. He saves some grains for sowing in future. Plough within what you earn from the *sadhana.* Do not go around bragging about it.

But remember, you cannot take a single step on this path if there is worldliness in you. All *sadhana* is meaningless if you have worldliness in you. If your mind is attracted to the fleeting pleasures of the world and is full of greed and lust, then all *spiritual* discipline will be hypocritical. Again, cleverness, manipulativeness, blackmail, bargaining, self-righteous demanding, pushing, can bear no fruit here. The *samsari* mind uses the same worldly tools to 'get' God, but it will not work. Ultimately, this worldliness within you has to end and God is always there. You know, once Rabia, the great *Sufi* saint, was listening to a sermon by another *Sufi* who kept on saying, "Whoever knocks at the door continually, it will be opened to him." Finally, after listening to many such sermons, she asked, "How long will you say, it will be opened? The door has never been shut."
By the time Babaji had finished, a large part of the day was over.
D: *Arre* Babaji, just look at the time!
Babaji: When you come to a *guru,* never come with other agendas and tight schedules.This Truth is *Bhagavati's prasada.* You should be ready to receive it when She offers it.

189. IS WEALTH AN IMPEDIMENT ON THIS PATH ?

D: Babaji, is wealth an impediment on this path?
Babaji: Simplicity will make a *sadhaka* humble. Materialism,

consumerism and living in things and objects are a great impediment on this path. It is the grossest manifestation of the ego. Material objects and things consume your energy. They have a 'will' of their own and will demand your attention. If for example, you have a TV in your house, it will demand to be used.

D: But Babaji, there are kings and wealthy persons who have attained God in the lap of luxury.

Babaji: There have also been poor people who have attained God.Why does your mind search out the examples that suit you? All kinds of people, from all walks of life, have experienced the final Truth. The 'emptying' and purity of the inner mind is all that matters.

D: You mean, you may live in wealth but the wealth should not live in you.

Babaji: Yes, but do you have the *viveka- buddhi* to figure out where you stand? I would caution a *sadhaka* against any form of materialism and ostentation, because it numbs sensitivity and produces physical sloth. Pre-occupation with gross material things can take away your subtle energies and inner strength and make you weak. Any weakness, be it physical, mental or emotional is a great hurdle on this Path. Pomp and show, wealth and glamour may increase self-importance but make you shallow. Every once in a way, just as an exercise, you can check out how enslaved you are to the things that money can buy. Once you have won the battle, you may throw off the armour but till then be careful.

To live in poverty also means to not crave for any kind of security, to be free of the need to provide for the future. It is a sign of child-like and complete surrender to God. You know the story of a princess who insisted that she would only marry a poor *Sufi*. The king, her father, was forced to visit mosques and *dargahs* to find her a match of her choice. Finally, they saw a poor mendicant praying in the mosque. The princess agreed to marry him. On reaching his house, she saw that he lived in a spartan manner but in one corner of the house she espied a piece of bread.

'What is that?' she asked her mendicant husband.

'O, that is a piece of bread that I have saved from yesterday. Let us now eat it together', said the *Sufi*.

'O God,' she said, I seem to have made a mistake. One who saves for the morrow must lack faith in *Allah's* ability to provide and look after his children. I have erred in the choice of a husband!'

Babaji continued: You know the saying – 'When I had no teeth, He provided milk. Won't he give bread when I have teeth?'

Of course, you must understand that these stories are not to encourage laziness but to reveal what a *sadhaka's* state of mind should be. It means devote your energies totally to the *sadhana* without fear of the morrow. If you do not have right understanding, the teachings will be lost on you. If you use the teachings to justify your stand, your weaknesses and prejudices; the teachings will be lost on you.

190. UNIVERSAL GOODWILL

To a disciple who was criticizing someone –

Babaji: If you think ill of others, it is immaterial whether your ill will actually harms them or not, but it will certainly sully and corrode your inner being. A sullied, stained mind is the cause of all sorrow. That is why one of the names of Bhagavati is *"maitryadivasanalabhya'* – The seeker must have *maitribhava* or feeling of friendliness towards all. Goodness, sheer goodness is a great boon on this path. The seeker should ignore the evil in the world and align to the good; he should rejoice in the joys of others and help those who are in pain. You know we have a saying – 'Good and evil seen in others will rub off on you but seen in yourself, it will leave you.' Therefore, see the good in others and the evil in yourself. One simple exercise you can do, to increase this feeling of universal friendliness, is to recite the following *shloka* daily at bed time –

सर्वेऽपि सुखिनः सन्तु सर्वे सन्तु निरामयाः ।
सर्वे भद्राणि पश्यन्तु मा कश्चिद्दुःखभाग्भवेत् ॥
॥ॐ शान्तिः शान्तिः शान्तिः ॥

Let all beings be happy, let all beings be in a disease free state.
Let all have the auspicious vision of Life,
Let there be no sorrow anywhere.
Let there be peace, peace, and peace.

191. THE POWER OF FAITH

D: Babaji, to me you are like God.

Babaji: My dear, it is your faith and receptivity, and not what I am, that makes it so.

Let me tell you a story –

A *sadhu* came to a village and started living under a tree. A devoted boy began to look after him. At first, he brought him a meal a day, and then two meals a day. As time passed, he started cleaning the ground where the *sadhu* sat and organizing his daily *puja*. Later, anticipating the rains, he built a small shelter around him. Then, he also assumed the responsibility of keeping it clean. The *sadhu* continued with his worship undisturbed.

Seeing the young boy's single-minded devotion, the villagers and skeptics started taunting and jeering at the boy for bestowing gurudom on an unknown person. 'You know nothing of his background, caste or lineage - what makes you waste your life on this *guru* who does not teach you or even speak to you', they said. Not heeding their taunts, the boy continued with his *seva*. He had by now even moved in with the *guru*.

Years passed by and one day, the *guru* passed away. The villagers gathered around and caustically asked the boy - 'so my dear, what did you get out of this *seva*? If your *guru* had such great powers, he should be able to come back from the dead and sit up right now, alive and kicking.' In exasperation, the boy went and whispered in the ears of the corpse, 'Sire, I have full faith in you, but just once, to shut up these ignorant villagers, can you not come back to life and sit up. Please do this for my sake, this last time.' The corpse immediately sat up, straight and erect. The dumbfounded villagers looked in awe and wonderment, and quietly left. The *guru* looked at the disciple and said - 'it is not my powers, but your faith that is responsible for this miracle.' So saying, he again fell dead.

Babaji continued : *'mano to devata, na mano to patthar!'* If you have faith, a stone image becomes an icon; if not, it is just a piece of stone.

192. A GREAT LEAP FORWARD

D: So then, this path is nothing but a study of your self in its different dimensions is it?

Babaji: Yes. In addition, each dimension of your self is governed by different rules.

देह बनायो जानवर, मनवा में शैतान ।
स्वयं प्रभुजी है बिरजे, हृदय कमल में आप ॥

The body and it's needs have to be treated like a pet animal - one is not cruel to one's pet, but is careful not to over indulge it. The mind is to be handled as one would a devil. You have to see through its game of self-deception and self-preservation and skillfully and intelligently extricate yourself from its hold. Do not be lenient with your mind. Do not spare it, as you would not spare a devil. Finally, Ishwar Himself resides in the lotus of the heart. Try to be one with Him. When you thus learn to handle the different dimensions of your personality, you will become integrated; that is the purpose of *yoga sadhana.*

D: Babaji, these analogies are so convincing and easy to understand but so difficult to live by.

Babaji: Identifying or operating from the ego is the chief problem. Stop identifying with this mind-body complex, this limited personality, and you will take a great leap forward.

193. AHAMKARA

D: Babaji, how does one deal with this *ahamkara?*
Babaji: *'A'* is the first letter of the alphabet and *'ha'* is the last. All that there is, is only the *akara* or form of this *aham.* Therefore, you do not have to crush your *ahamkara,* you have to only expand it. Try to expand your 'I' consciousness to include everything and everyone.

194. THE EGO IS ESSENTIAL FOR SELF-PROTECTION BUT NOT FOR SELF-DECEPTION

Babaji (in a trance like state). *Beta,* this ego is a very useful thing. That is why it is given to us. Only, we have to know how to use it. What happens most of the time, is that, it uses us.
This ego is like a lion; powerful, grand and ferocious. Why do you think my Goddess is called *'Sherawali'* or riding a lion? Why do you think she is called *'shrimadsimhasaneshvari'* in the *Lalitasahasranama?* It is because, She is a master of this lion of the ego - guiding it and disciplining it. But in case of us lesser mortals, we are tyrannized by this lion, fearfully waiting at its beck and call. We do not ride the lion, but are driven by it! We do not sit astride it, in full command, but in fact, it chases us. We are slaves to the ego. But you do not have to get rid of the ego. Simply learn to wield it judiciously and skillfully and absolutely never allow it to use you. You be the ringmaster. You are the ringmaster!
D: But Babaji, all masters and scriptures insist that this evil ego must be annihilated.
Babaji : The ego is essential for self-protection. *'Aham'* or 'I' in the form of the undivided psyche keeps together the mind-body complex and is the basis for a healthy self-esteem. If this *'aham '* would not be there, your very survival would have been threatened.

Listen to this story -
Once upon a time, there was a Cobra, dreaded and feared by all. Many innocent people had died because of his venom. One day, a sage was passing through the jungle. As was his habit, the Cobra was about to bite the sage but was caught in time by the master. The reptile pleaded for life. The sage agreed on one condition, - that he would not bite indiscriminately. The Cobra promised to lead a life of non-violence.
Days passed by and the Cobra kept his word, even at the cost of threat to his life. Children pelted stones at him, passers by carelessly stamped his tail, and insecure, fearful villagers beat him with sticks even when he was lying quietly. But the Cobra continued to practice forbearance; till even the maintainence of his body became difficult. Sensing his grave state, the sage reappeared. He said, 'I asked you to refrain from biting indiscriminately; I did not ask you to stop hissing.'
Babaji continued: You have to learn to wield this ego rightly for your survival. The ego is for self-protection and not self-deception. But out of perversion and wrong understanding, what was essentially to protect one's self, only serves to divide, injure and destroy. When the ego takes the form of self-importance and self-deception, it is a poison. It is this poisonous, divisive ego, that all saints and masters ask you to vanquish. Not only for *sadhana,* but in life too, happy is the person free of the poisonous ego.
D: Babaji, did you also have to conquer this poisonous ego?
Babaji: Of course, that is what *sadhana* is all about. You know, once during my *sadhana* period, I saw a huge snake lying in front of me. My first reaction was to run in fear. But I realized that it could run faster than I could. Therefore, I simply closed my eyes and continued to meditate. For many days, it continued to appear when I sat in meditation. One day, when I got up from meditation, I saw a coil of ash in front of me. That cobra was the symbol of my ego. When my ego was burnt, it

became a heap of ashes. It is vital to remember, that you are both all important and not important at all. Truth will always be balanced on this razor's edge.

D: Babaji, how difficult it is to understand and implement these things.

Babaji: Yes right understanding *(viveka)* is difficult. Only through *sadhana* can this ego be rightly understood and its poison destroyed. Only *sadhana* can translate into *'viveka'*. Intellectual understanding and bookish knowledge is of little use.

D: Then what should one do Babaji?

Babaji: Do your *sadhana* and don't worry. I am there. When the driver is there, the passengers do not have to worry. (To another disciple) Do you understand heroine? This one here thinks that she is a big heroine. This is ego - what else?

D: So what should I do Babaji?

Babaji: Nothing. You have come to *Bhagavati*. She will do what needs to be done.

195. SUBTLE EGO

Observing a student who was morally upright and good.

Babaji: This goodness is a greater trap than evil. Here, a subtle ego cleverly masquerades all the time. Self-righteousness is even more incurable than unrighteousness.

196. SURRENDER TO GOD IN HUMILITY

Often in an ecstatic mood, Babaji would recite *stotras*.

One of his favorite lines was *'natanam jananam samastam pradatrim'*

Babaji: 'To those whose heads are bowed down in humility and not puffed up with their own pride, She gives everything.' To those who surrender to Her, to those who have no complaints in life, She gives everything. To accept your lot in life without complaints, is a sign of great humility. Look at the *Sufi* saint *Rabia*.

D: Who was she, what about her?
Babaji: Rabia lived in the 12th century in Turkestan. She was sold off to a rich man and lived as his slave. She faced untold physical and mental trauma and abuse, working day and night to keep body and soul together. Yet she never lost sight of her aim- to become one with God. After a day's drudgery, she would lock herself in the room and pray. Once, her master hearing her soulful prayers and peeped through the curtain to find her bathed in divine light. That very moment, he begged forgiveness for all his atrocities and set her free.
Babaji continued: Have no complaints in life, for God looks after all His children. Through the thick and thin of life, one should not lose sight of the ultimate goal of God realization. That is real humility. Whimpering, whining, grumbling, blaming...these only take you away from God. To accept God's Will, is the highest form of humility.

197. COME WITH YOUR HEAD BENT (IN HUMILITY)

Babaji (welcoming a devotee)**:** Please come in
D: Ouch! Babaji your hut has such a low roof, that each time I come here, I hit myself on the head.
Babaji: When you come to *Bhagavati*, you must come with your head bent (in humility).

198. INITIATION

To a disciple who had just been initiated –
Babaji: Bury deep inside you, this seed of spirituality, so that it may flower. A seed held in the palm of the hands, to show off to the world, will only be blown away by the wind. Buried in the womb of the earth, it flowers. Do not wear your spirituality on your sleeve.

199. DIKSHA OR INITIATION

D: Babaji, what is *diksha* or initiation?

Babaji: It is a process whereby the *guru* gives *(diyate)* positive and higher energies to the aspirant and takes away or destroys (*kshiyate*) his/her negative energies and impurities. It is like a booster dose. The *guru* gives his energies and vision to the disciple. It is a rebirth for the disciple, who will now see life with a renewed consciousness and insight.

Once *diksha* is given, the aspirant becomes a disciple and is connected to the *gurumandala* forever. Then you may go where you want, pursue the *sadhana* or not, but the seed has been sown forever and the protective net of the *gurus* is thrown around you. This is an *akshaya bija* or indestructible seed. You will carry it with you from birth to birth. At death, the *guru* alone waits to guide you.

D: So Babaji, how do you decide who has to be initiated?

Babaji (beating his head and laughing)**:** *Laddu hai* (you ball of sweet). I decide nothing. The *gurumandala* decides. I am their servant. When you are ready, the Force descends. Many people approach me and ask for *diksha*. However, until their time comes, the Force will not descend. See, how each one of you has been initiated at different times.

D: So once we are initiated, is the role of the *guru* over?

Babaji: Just by being admitted to school, is the process of education over? There are many kinds of *diksha,* ending in the final initiation.

D: So then, *diksha* is when the *guru* gives you a *mantra* is it?

Babaji: The imparting of a *mantra* is only one form of initiation. A *guru* has many weapons in his armory. A *guru* transmits energies through the eyes i.e. through a look, a touch, a thought or a *mantra*. Often he may use a combination of different methods of transmission. I transmit best through the look, the touch and through the transmission of a *mantra.* Once a *mantra* is given to you, it repeats itself in your body. You have to be aware of it. Also, there are many levels of *diksha*. There is *anavi diksha, shambhavi diksha, shakta diksha* and

nirupaya diksha depending on the stage at which the disciple is. Each one is subtler than the previous one.
D : What does that mean?
Babaji (smiling)**:** You will know, when you get it.

200. MEDITATE ON THE FEET OF THE GURU

Babaji would often come home and intuitively know that we had been neglecting our *sadhana,* or had lost equanimity for some reason, or acquired a mundane consciousness, being steeped in our day-to-day affairs. He would chide us sternly or feel pensive and say *'ghasar rahi ho neeche'* - you are sliding down.' Sometimes he would just touch you and know what was your state of mind. To disciples, this was like an exam failed.
D: Babaji, I panic when you chide me like this.
Babaji: What to do *beta?* When a man has only a few coins in his pocket, he keeps on checking if they are there. He does not want to lose them. See, today I feel that your *dhyana* has moved away from the *guru charan* – the feet of the *guru.*
D (Dejected and panic stricken)**:** What should I do now?
Babaji (Laughing)**:** *Arre,* if you have left the *guru's* feet, what else can you do? Just catch hold of them. That's all. See how simple it is.
(Singing away)
मनश्चेन्न लग्नं गुरोरंघ्रिपद्मे ततः किं ततः किं ततः किं ततः किम् ।
शरीरं सुरूपं तथा वा कलत्रं यशश्चारु चित्रं धनं मेरुतुल्यम् ॥
मनश्चेन्न लग्नं गुरोरंघ्रिपद्मे ततः किं ततः किं ततः किं ततः किम् ।
The body looks handsome, the wife attractive, fame spreads far and wide, wealth enormous and stable like mount Meru; but of what consequence are all these, if the mind is not riveted in devotion to the lotus feet of the Guru, the Teacher? Really, of what use is all this, what use, what use?

201. SUPREME INDEPENDENCE

D: Babaji, why did *Gurumaharaj* ask you to leave him after your *sadhana* period was over?

Babaji: Ultimately, you have to be free of the *guru* also. This path is about independence.

Let me tell you a story –

A man was very attached to his wife. He could not live without her for a moment. One day, he went to a *guru* and confided his problem. The *guru* simply plucked a *tulsi*(basil) leaf and asked him to eat it. And lo! the man left his wife and started living in the *ashram* and doing *guru seva.* When his wife heard of this, she was intrigued. She too wanted to meet the *guru.* On meeting him, she asked him – 'What is it that you have given him? I too would like to have that.' The *guru* plucked another leaf and gave it to her. She ate that and even left the *guru!*

Babaji continued: Of course, physical distance from the *guru,* does not mean an emotional distancing, a lack of love or an absence of surrender at the master's feet. The *guru* is the Center of your Consciousness. In essence, how can one ever move away from Him.

D: I do not think I can ever leave you, even physically. Babaji, please read this little parable, that I have written to express this feeling.

Babaji (reads)**:** You are not yet ready to leave the *guru.*

202. WHAT ARE THE 'PASSING MARKS' IN THIS JOURNEY

D: Babaji, one reads of many *lokas* and realms that have to be conquered and many levels of expanding consciousness, that can be reached. But what are the 'passing marks' in this journey?

Babaji: Just the attitude that – 'May my Consciousness always be anchored at the feet of the *guru.*' That's all.

203. ALL ILLUSIONS MUST BE BROKEN

A disciple was disappointed.

Babaji: Disillusionment with the world is very good. To find Truth, all illusions must be broken. Why, even if you are disillusioned with me, that will be a good thing for you!

204. THE DARKNESS WITHIN

Babaji's *ashram* had no electricity. That darkness taught us many things. Babaji would compare it to the darkness within and tell us –

Babaji: The only way to conquer the fear of darkness is through complete acceptance of the darkness, by being with it wholly, by not resisting it or running away from it. If you can do that, then slowly you will start seeing things in the dark; a light will emerge. The same holds true for the darkness within. It is the darkness of your ego, of ignorance. Understand it. To know your ignorance is Knowledge. Honest acceptance of the darkness in you, is the first ray of light. Be with the darkness of your ego in attentive acceptance, and slowly the light of awareness will emerge. This attentiveness is only the light. Once this inner light appears, its luminousness can put to shame a thousand lamps. It is a million times more than the light of even the sun and the moon and countless such heavenly bodies. Therefore, the Goddess is referred to as '*udyadbhanusahasrabha* – bright like a thousand suns.'

Let me tell you the story of the *Sufi* saint Rabia –

Once, she was seated in her room in deep meditation when, her friend, who happened to see the full moon in all its beauty called out, "Hey come and see the light outside." Rabia said, "Why don't you come 'In' and see the light within that I am seeing?"

(Although at that time, we could not comprehend fully, what the effulgence of that inner light must be, such interactions with Babaji, whetted our appetite for Truth and inspired us to get serious about our inner search.)

205. THIS HUMAN BIRTH IS A RARE CHANCE, DON'T WASTE IT

Babaji would often despair at how people wasted their life, in running after sense pleasures and holding on to their negativity and prejudices.

Babaji: Precious life is passing by and humankind fritters it away in shallow, superficial pursuits, trivial worries and gross sense pleasures. As a moth consumed by flames, humanity is consumed by its lusts.

What a waste of life – *'malayachal ki bhilni chandana det jalay!'* The *bhilni* or tribal woman, takes for granted, the sandalwood jungle that she lives in, and using its precious wood for her ordinary chores. What a shame!

This human birth is priceless. It is offers a unique opportunity for *mukti* – liberation. Neither God, nor animal nor any aspect of Nature, has the opportunity that Man has. This human birth is a rare chance – do not waste it, do not take it for granted.

206. YOUR BODY HAS BEEN DESIGNED TO DO SADHANA

D: Babaji, I really find it very difficult to find the time for *sadhana* because of my familial duties and professional commitments.

Babaji: This human birth is given to find God. The human anatomy is designed to raise subtle energy upwards – Godwards. Human evolution is an ascent – a rising upward vertically. That is why *Bhagavati* is called *'chidagnikunda sambhuta devakarya samudyata* – She is born in the Fire of the *manipura chakra* and then rises upward to accomplish the divine work of awakening.' The vertical human spine, with centres of Consciousness located along it, is designed for ascent, and evolution and raising of energies to the higher centres. This precious opportunity is not available to plants or animals. Nature offers many opportunities for awakening, in simple day to day acts like sleeping and breathing. But nothing is possible without attentive and conscious awareness. Without awareness, these potential treasures lie undiscovered.

D: Why is awareness important? Is not a treasure, a treasure?

Babaji: If you have a blank cheque in your pocket and you do not know about it, what is the use? Awareness is a torch that reveals, cleans and actualises.

Take sleep for example. Often you get up with the feeling that 'I slept very well' or 'I did not sleep well.' Who was it that observed this state in you? If you were to be aware, even in sleep, of this 'Watcher'; then you could be said to be in a meditative state. So, every day, Nature gives you this opportunity to know yourself.

Then take the act of breathing. You take 21,600 breaths per day. Each one of these is a glorious opportunity to awaken. Between each inhalation and exhalation, there is a subtle gap. In this small gap, wherein you breathe neither in nor out, the mind becomes vacant. Through this gap the Self peeps. By practice, you have to learn to become more alert, so that you can observe this cessation of breath, and hence of thought. As you practice, this gap will go on expanding and you will dissolve in that emptiness and void. Motion *(gati)* and inertia *(sthiti)* are both forms of energy and life is an interplay of both these. If you become aware of that, you will be connected to the Source. Nothing in the world is continuous. Many such gaps are provided by Nature, to reveal the hidden Self. Besides the breath, there are the gaps between your desires, gaps between your thoughts, gaps between words, between movements and actions. All these have to be carefully watched, to grasp that subtle revelation. But because our sensibilities have become gross, these subtleties are lost. We have to therefore fine-tune our instruments, to raise the level of sensitivity.

So, if time is your problem, do the *ajapa japa*. Every breath is reciting the *hamsa mantra*. That is why *Devi* is *'hamsini'* because she is the very breath in this body. She rides on the breath. She is also called '*marali*' or '*mandagama*' because she moves slowly, gracefully and leisurely throughout the whole body. The '*hamsa mantra*' is constantly repeated in your body. Listen carefully; and with every inhalation, you will hear, the '*ham*' sound, and with every exhalation, the '*sah*' sounds. With repeated awareness of this *hamsa mantra,* it will convert into *soham* - I am that. Every breath is reminding you, 'I am that, I am that.' It is a *mantra (japa)* that does not require 'doing' *(ajapa)*, because it is always 'happening'. Whenever you are traveling or waiting for the bus, just observe your breath, be with it until you dissolve in it. This will be a very potent *sadhana*. Moreover, it will not take up time in your busy schedule. See, even as I talk to you now, I experience the *japa* happening inside me. So also, it happens inside all. Just be aware of it.

207. O MAN, BE ALERT, FOR LIFE PASSES BY

D: Babaji, what is the right age to begin *sadhana*?

Babaji: This must be achieved in youth. *'buddha tota kya padhega* -what can an old parrot learn?' Unless you begin at a young age, what can you achieve when you are old and ailing? While the senses and the body are strong, search within. (Singing away) – *vachi bola datta nama, savdhan, savdhan!* (To a disciple) Today is *Datta Jayanti.*

Why don't you sing that beautiful bhajan for me?

D: सावधान, सावधान; वाचे बोला दत्त नाम; सावधान, सावधान ॥

O man, be alert, be alert. Chant the sacred name of Datta.

Be aware,be aware (for life passes by).

> दहा वर्षे बालपण, वीस वर्षे तारूण्य
> अंगी चढे अभिमान, नसे स्वरूपाची जाण ॥
> सावधान, सावधान; वाचे बोला दत्त नाम; सावधान, सावधान ॥

Childhood for ten years, at twenty comes youth,

Strutting pride engulfs you; as blissfully oblivious of your

True Nature (you are),
O man, be alert, be alert. Chant the sacred name of Datta.
Be aware, be aware (for life passes by).

> तिसाची होय भरती, कन्या पुत्र लाभ होती ।
> शांतीत पडल्या भ्रांति, नसे स्वरूपाची कीर्ती ॥
> सावधान, सावधान; वाचे बोला दत्त नाम; सावधान, सावधान ॥

Enter the terrible thirties; wealth, wife and child are gained,
Peace is forever shattered, oblivious of the glory of your True Nature (you are),
O man, be alert, be alert. Chant the sacred name of Datta.
Be aware, be aware (for life passes by).

> चाळीस वर्षे झाली, डोळया चाळीशी आली ।
> नेत्रासी भूल पडली, येता दिसे न जवळी ॥
> सावधान, सावधान; वाचे बोला दत्त नाम; सावधान, सावधान ॥

Ah you have now reached forty, the face is bespectacled,
Confused is the vision, and short sighted too.
O man, be alert, be alert. Chant the sacred name of Datta.
Be aware, be aware (for life passes by).

> पन्नासाची होय भरती, दंतपंगती हलती ।
> शामकेश शुभ्र होती, त्याला म्हातारा म्हणती ॥
> सावधान, सावधान; वाचे बोला दत्त नाम; सावधान, सावधान ॥

Welcome to the fifties; teeth are shaking and quaking,
The black crown of hair has turned grey,
Now, referred to as 'the old man' (you are),
O man, be alert, be alert. Chant the sacred name of Datta.
Be aware, be aware (for life passes by).

> साठाची बुद्धी नाठी, हाती घेऊनिया काठी ।
> वसवस लागे पाठी, त्याला हासती पोरटी ॥
> सावधान, सावधान; वाचे बोला दत्त नाम; सावधान, सावधान ॥

Sixty and senile, and supported by a walking stick,
Irritable and laughed at by children you are,

O man, be alert, be alert. Chant the sacred name of Datta.
Be aware, be aware (for life passes by).

> सत्तरीच्या विवंचना, मग होती यातना ।
> बसविता उठवेना, उठविता चालवेना ॥
> सावधान, सावधान; वाचे बोला दत्त नाम; सावधान, सावधान ॥

O the agony and pain of the seventies,
O, the agonising effort to sit, stand or move.
O man, be alert, be alert. Chant the sacred name of Datta.
Be aware,be aware (for life passes by).

> चार विसा मिळोनी ऐशी होती, मग झाला देशोदेशी ।
> जळेवीण मत्स्य जैसा, जीव होतो कासाविशी ॥
> सावधान, सावधान; वाचे बोला दत्त नाम; सावधान, सावधान ॥

Four times twenty and restless
Like a fish out of water, is the anguish of your soul.
O man, be alert, be alert. Chant the sacred name of Datta.
Be aware,be aware (for life passes by).

> नऊवर दिले पूज्य, एक राहिले पूज्य ।
> म्हणतसे माझे माझे, आता काय आहे तुझे ॥
> सावधान, सावधान; वाचे बोला दत्त नाम; सावधान, सावधान ॥

Nine and zero-ninety, and zero is what is left,
'Me' and 'mine' you had chanted, now who or what is 'yours.'
O man, be alert, be alert. Chant the sacred name of Datta.
Be aware, be aware (for life passes by).

> राजहंस उडोनि गेला, देह कोरडा पडला ।
> जन म्हणती मेला मेला, मोठया आनंदाने नेला ॥
> सावधान, सावधान; वाचे बोला दत्त नाम; सावधान, सावधान ।

Life breath has flown off, lifeless lies the body,
Cheerfully they say, 'O he is dead. He is dead!'
as they prepare for your final departure.
O man, be alert, be alert. Chant the sacred name of Datta.
Be aware, be aware (for life passes by).

आता म्हणे गुरूराज, सोडा संसाराची आस ।
सांगतो मी सज्जनास, धरा सद्गुरुची कास ॥
सावधान, सावधान; वाचे बोला दत्त नाम; सावधान, सावधान ॥

Now atleast, says gurumaharaj, give up desire for this illusive life,
O, you high born ones, hold on to the feet of the sadgurus.
O man, Be alert, be alert. Chant the sacred name of Datta.
Be aware, be aware (for life passes by).

~

On Gurus...

Name, fame and fortune,
Good friends and relations,
Many are the treasures on the journey of life,
But blessed are they, who have found a Master,
A thousand fold more blessed they,
who have merged with Him.

~

208. PRECIOUS ARE THE FEET OF THE MASTER

Babaji: So, what is the most precious possession that you have?

D: I don't know.[1]

Babaji: The most precious possession I have is my *Gurumaharaj.*

(Goes into a trance like state and bursts into an Urdu poem)

Tere naqsh-e-pa se qadam qadam,
woh maqam-e-sabr-o-raza mila
Tere dar se jo bhi mila mujhe, mere hausle se siwa mila

Simply by following your divine footsteps, I have found the Eternal Grace. Whatever I have got from your doorstep, is much much more than I deserve.

209. IS A GURU NECESSARY ?

D: Babaji is a *guru* necessary?

Babaji: Howsoever much a woman may decorate herself, with lipstick and make-up, till she finds a husband, she cannot have a child. If you want to enjoy the child of Truth, you must have a *guru*. It is he who impregnates you with the living Truth.

210. WHO IS A GURU ?

Conversations with Babaji were often in the form of soliloquies. He would talk, or as he said, *Gurumaharaj* would talk. "Even I am listening to him, as you are listening to me", he would say,

Babaji: *Guru* does not mean a particular man or woman. *Guru* means the light of truth and knowledge – *'sat-chit-ananda'*.

211. ARE YOU A GURU ?

D: Babaji, are you a *guru*?

Babaji: I am just a tap. They, the higher powers turn me on, and the Force descends. At other times, I am just like any one else. Try to sense the Force and not this ordinary personality. Tune in to the Force.

---

1 The 'D' in all conversations refers to Disciple.

212. AWAKEN THE GURU WITHIN

Babaji: The *guru* is like soap. While he is there, use him. However, the real progress will happen only after he is gone. Only then, will you learn independence. Do you know why I kiss you on the forehead, between the eyebrows, when you bow down to me? So that your *ajna chakra* is activated and the inner guru is awakened. Eventually you have to rely on the inner Self alone.

213. TIME SPENT WITH THE MASTER

D: Babaji, I enjoy everything in your company and am contented doing whatever you do. It is all an illuminating, learning experience.

Babaji (Laughing)**:** Don't trap a poor Babaji in flattering words.Actually, we have a saying that, 'the warmth of the sun must be taken on the back, the warmth of a fire, on the stomach. But the *guru's* warmth must be enjoyed from the front, the back and from wherever possible'. Time spent with the master must never be calculated or rationed. Never go to a teacher with limited time. You have to be ready, when the teacher is inspired and in a mood to teach. Besides, these teachings are not mine, they come from above; even I do not know, when they will start flowing. All the time spent with the master, is a learning experience, if you have the sensitivity.

214. I LOVE YOU

D: Babaji, I love you.

Babaji: And who am I?

D: I do not know.

Babaji: Your very Self.

215. ALONE WITH BABAJI

D: Babaji, when I am with you, I feel as if I am all alone, by myself, in a state of beautiful solitude.

Babaji: Yes, I am your Self.

216. GURU IS EVERYTHING

D: Babaji, sometimes I feel you are like my brother, sometimes like my husband, sometimes like my father…
Babaji: Yes and sometimes you will see your child in me. I am all relationships. I am the platform from which all relationships spring. I am your Self.

217. LOVE THE GURU

Babaji: So, when will you come again to the *ashram?*
D: When should I come Babaji?
Babaji: There are no 'shoulds' here.
'Yeh pyar ka sauda hai'. This is a pact of love, not duty.

218. I AM NOT A RELATIONSHIP

D: Babaji, have you any idea how much I have been missing you, in your absence?
Babaji: To remember me, is your 'work', your *sadhana.* However, try to see me as the *guru tattva* and not as this person. I am not this person. If you see Truth in me, I am of use to you; but if you see only the ordinary personality in me, then that is all that you will get. It will be just one more relationship in your life, with its pleasures and pains. I am not a relationship – I am the platform, from which you can understand all relationships.

219. BABAJI, I MISS YOU!

D: Babaji, I miss you all the time. Don't you also miss me?
Babaji: How can I miss you? You are always with me. You know that verse of Ghalib – *'jab jara gardan jhuka li, dekh li tasveere yaar* – I have to only bend my head and there I see you (in my heart).'

220. LIMBS OF THE SAME BODY

Once, when Babaji returned from the *ashram* –

D: Babaji, yesterday I had a very elevating experience.

Babaji: I know.

D: How?

Babaji: If one limb of your body feels something, won't you know?

221. DOES THAT SADHAKA HAVE A GURU ?

D: Babaji, does that *sadhaka* whom you were talking to, have a *guru*?

Babaji: How should I know?

D: Why did you not ask him?

Babaji: Can you ask a highborn woman whether she is married or how she woos her beloved? Similarly, the *guru-shishya* relationship is a very private and intimate relationship, of deep friendship. Moreover, if that intimate relationship is not there, then the transmission will not happen.

(Babaji himself shared an informal and friendly relationship with his disciples. Many times while taking leave, he would hold out his hand and say *"dosti pukki hai ki nahi* - are we best friends or not?")

222. GURU AND SHISHYA ARE ONE

(At a disciple's house, a few days before Babaji passed away.)

D: Babaji, please eat this apple.

Babaji: Why do you waste so much money on these costly fruits?

D (laughing)**:** Babaji, when will you stop counting money and economising?

Babaji: (Accepts the apple. After taking a bite offers it to the disciple.)

D: Babaji, that is for you.

Babaji: And, when will you understand that I am you.

(Babaji often worshipped his disciples while initiating them. Once on the banks of the Mandakini river at Rudra Prayag, he lovingly washed the face of all his disciples and kissed them between the eyebrows. These simple acts, he would say, were ways of initiating the student and uplifting his/her consciousness. As a rule, he would put *kumkum* on their forehead and at the throat center (*vishuddi chakra*) to awaken their consciousness. Each time he applied the *tika,* he would affectionately kiss on the forehead. Babaji would say – 'I kiss all that I love, be it disciples or gods or books.'

223. YOU ARE MY VERY FORM

Babaji (To a disciple, who had offered his services as a driver, for the *ashram* work.)**:** Here, take these 1500/- rupees; this is *Bhagavati's prasad* for you. You are not my driver, you are my disciple. *Guru* and *shishya* are one. You are my very form.
(Babaji would carry this feeling and cook for disciples, fold their bedding, help in simple household chores and even wash their toilets and bathrooms! While setting up the *ashram* at Telbaila, he would himself dig the land for hours, to clear it of boulders and stones. To watch his intense involvement in these little acts, was itself a learning experience.)

224. BABAJI, YESTERDAY I DREAMT OF YOU

D: Babaji, yesterday I dreamt of you, but I cannot remember what you said.
Babaji: When the *guru* appears in a dream and his words are not remembered, it means that the purity is lacking.
D: Babaji, does *Gurumaharaj* ever come in your dreams?
Babaji: No, I have never dreamt of him. He talks to me directly, here (pointing to his heart).

225. GURU SEVA

D: Babaji, I just feel like cooking for you, washing your clothes, and doing a million other chores for you.

Babaji: This selfless love is good for you. It purifies you and melts the ego. Even Truth surrenders to selfless, egoless love. That is why *Bhagavati* is called *'bhakti vashya, bhakti gamya* – She is enslaved to selfless devotion, She goes to selfless Love.' As such, by doing *guru seva,* you are only helping yourself to become pure and selfless. In effect, the *shishya* does not do any *seva.* It is only the *guru,* who does *seva* by working day and night, for the upliftment of the *shishya's* consciousness.

226. THE GURU - SHISHYA RELATIONSHIP

D: So Babaji, what is the *dharma* of a *shishya*? What is his duty?
Babaji: Quite simply – to love the teacher. Love, without any interference from the ego and without judging. This love automatically inspires a disciple to walk on the path shown by the teacher.

There are three types of *guru-seva* (service to the master). The first, is to look after the material needs of the master. Secondly, to give the time and energy to do the simple chores of his life like e.g. washing or mending his clothes, cooking for him or even dedicating oneself to any educational, spiritual or missionary work that the *guru* undertakes. And the last and most important form of *guru-seva* is, to walk on the spiritual path shown by the *guru.* These three forms of service to the *guru* happen naturally if there is pure love for the teacher.

Once you have accepted some one as your teacher, set aside all judgment, because what you judge is the personality and a personality will always be a combination of light and dark. See the Truth in the teacher and not the raiments of his personality. Look at the Truth that the master is pointing to.

Singing a verse from The *Avadhoota Gita* -

बालस्य वा विषयभोगरतस्य वापि
मूर्खस्य सेवकजनस्य गृहस्थितस्य ।
एतद्गुरोः किमपि नैव न चिंतनीयं
रत्नं कथं त्यजति कोऽप्यशुचौ प्रतिष्ठम् ॥

Do not think lightly of a teacher that he is a child, a fool,
a profligate, a servant or a householder.
Does anyone give up a jewel,
merely because it lies in a quarry full of dirt?

D: But Babaji, there are rogues, charlatans, and fake *sadhus*, as you yourself have encountered in the Himalayas. How does one know that one has met one's *guru*?

Babaji: Once I asked the same question to *Gurumaharaj* and he said 'At whomsoever's feet you find peace and a cessation of craving, a coming to rest of the mind; know that person to be your *guru*.' You can take this simple test to check whether you are in the presence of your *guru*:

- Has the *guru* opened your eyes to the Truth and lifted the curtain of delusion that blinds your eyes,?

Then, that is your master.

- Does he fill your heart with peace/love and most importantly, a yearning for God?

Then, that is your master.

- Does he threaten your ego and make you question your preferences, prejudices and *agrahas*? Do you start looking inward?

Then, that is your master.

- Does the conflict and craving within you reduce and cease? Then, that is your master.
- Does your understanding and acceptance of people increase?

Then, that is your master.

- Does the teacher have any personal motive in guiding you, or, is love and your spiritual growth his only concern?

Then, that is your master.

Yes, there are rogues and charlatans, but you will always find the *guru* you deserve. At the same time, a *guru* is a mirror, not an idol. An idol is distant and imaginary. The *guru* is your Truth body. He points again and again, towards that center of your own Consciousness. He reaches you to yourself, while your idol will always take you away from yourself. That is why, it is important to be close to a teacher and share an intimacy and not a formal, social relationship with all its posing, and niceties and hypocrisy. Only love for the *guru* can make you shed your inhibitions and drop the 'mask.'

D: Shouldn't it be enough, to just walk on the path? Why is 'loving' the teacher important?

Babaji: Because love purifies, love melts the ego, love surrenders. Love will give you all the qualities of the heart that are required on this path. Love washes away that most poisonous thing called doubt. It washes away doubt in the existence of Truth, doubt in the master and his teachings. The teacher, the Truth and God are one; when you love the teacher you automatically love Truth and God and become one with them. Remember what the saint poet *Kabir* has said, '*prem gali ati sakari, tin mei dau na samay*' - The lane of Love is narrow - two cannot walk on it.' *Yeh rasta ekatva ki aur jane ka hai'* – This path is of going towards Oneness, to shed divisiveness, to become Whole and Integrated. Love is that very State. Nevertheless, you must love the Truth in the teacher. If you love the personality, then sooner or later you will feel impressed, awed and idolatrous or let down, disillusioned and disappointed. If you see the teacher as a person, then he becomes like countless others.

D: So what should my attitude to you be?

Babaji: The *shishya's* treasure is *guruseva* and *brahmacharya* or residing in the Self. Just love Me, live the Truth that I am pointing to and remember that I am not this person. That's all! Do not find faults with a teacher, disapprove of his work, or judge him by ordinary standards. You know, Mirabai's guru Ravidas was a cobbler. Once, people passed remarks about the kind of menial work that he did. *Mirabai,* being a queen, requested him to give up his lowly profession. He said, 'If I am an embarrassment to you, please do not take the trouble to come here. I have given you the *vidya*. Even if you practice that by yourself, you will attain.' Or take another example -

A *siddha* was sitting by the wayside. A king happened to pass by in a palanquin. The palanquin bearers needed help. Gruffly they asked the *siddha,* who looked like an ordinary beggar, to give a helping hand. Without any fuss, he obliged. But he could not keep pace with the others who were experts and did this task daily. They jeered and poked fun at him but he took it all patiently. Only when the king talked to him later, did he realise that here was a great master who understood Truth. Indeed, it is difficult to recognise a knower of Truth.

D: So, can this Truth not be culled from scriptures and books?

Babaji: Can the description of a tasty dish, satisfy your palate? How can living Truth be substituted by discursive discourse? Besides, this is a study of your individual self and not of a theory. Reading without doing any *sadhana* and without guidance from a teacher, is a complete waste of time. Neither the emperorship of the three worlds, nor the fruits of rigorous *tapas*, can compare to the magical awakening that happens in the presence of a master. You know, before I left for the Himalayas, I locked myself in a room for a year and read the *vedas, upanishads* and many other religious texts. At the end of this entire endeavor, I felt that books could not satisfy me. I wanted to find a person who had seen God and tasted Truth. That is why I left home.

D: So when you left home, did you not carry any books with you?

Babaji: I had only one book with me – The *Avadhoota Gita.*

D (hugging Babaji)**:** Now I do not have to worry about anything, because I have found a *guru.*

Babaji continued: But do not think that the *guru* will do *sadhana* for you. Don't expect the *guru* to put you into a state of *samadhi*. You yourself will have to do difficult *sadhanas*. A hungry man has to feed himself.

227. GURU'S WRATH

D: Babaji, why do you get so angry with me?

Babaji: Oh, blessed are they who taste the wrath of a teacher. The fire of that anger will wash all their impurities away. Remember how *Guru maharaj* beat me with a stick? It is the *guru's prasada.*

D (laughing)**:** Some *prasada* that is Babaji!

Babaji: The *guru* is like a potter who beats the clay from outside but supports it from within. He is not beating the pot, he is only shaping it.

228. GURUMANDALA

D: Babaji, what is a *gurumandala?*

Babaji: Literally it means a lineage of *gurus* beginning with your immediate *guru,* continuing into your great *guru,* great great *guru* and so on, and ending in *Shiva* himself. It is your spiritual ancestry. It is your spiritual inheritance, your spiritual genes. Just as every human being has parents, so also, everyone has a *guru.*

The *gurumandala* is a divine ladder to ascend to Truth. Just as in school you have kindergarten teachers, primary school teachers, and secondary school teachers and finally you have the principal; then there is a hierarchy of teachers for graduation, post graduation, doctoral studies, post doctoral studies and so on; similarly there is a ladder of spiritual teachers. There are *mantra gurus, mantreshvar gurus* and *mantra maheshvara gurus,* and thus the chain continues. Some are guides, some are prophets, some are messengers of Truth, some are *siddhas* and some are *avatars* or incarnations of God and so on. Each one is a vital link in that chain of Truth. This chain connects you to the ultimate Truth. Can you imagine how priceless and precious that chain is, for a man drowning in the sea of delusion called the world!

The *gurumandala* holds the collective force of the *tapas,* the *sadhanas,* the insights and spiritual attainments of many generations of *siddhas* in the lineage. Individual effort however great, is puny compared to this Collective Force and cannot attain the grand and priceless Truth without their grace. At the same time, each one of you adds to that Collective Force by the strength of your *sadhana.*

The *guru mandala* is a circuit or energy diagram connecting the center of your consciousness to the Consciousness of the *gurus.* But Consciousness is universal and so the Center of Consciousness can only be One. Therefore, *guru* and *shishya* are one.

Similarly, there are many such *guru mandalas* and ultimately all of them are connected to that great fount of Truth or Shiva. Therefore, in the final analysis, all *gurus* and *gurumandalas* are One. Yet, to you, your *guru* is important, like your parents. I often ask *Gurumaharaj* as to why my disciples are not able to connect with him, in spite of his stature and he would say, 'to them, you will always be the *guru*, not I.'

However, the *guru* reveals himself only when you are ready. Until then, s/he waits patiently. Can you imagine the patience of a *guru,* who waits for *yugas* (aeons) for you to wake up! See, I have been around in Bombay for so long and yet, of the millions in this city, only a few of you are my disciples, and each of you met me when you were ready. Not all spiritual aspirants belong to me. Even in a single family, not all the members belong to me. (Turning to a disciple) You belong to me, so does one of your daughters. Nevertheless, your younger daughter does not belong to me. However, she will find her *guru* in this very birth.

The *guru* and the *shishya* need each other. Just as the disciple pines for a *guru,* a *guru* also longs for the right disciple. If there is an intense desire in the disciple, the *guru* comes searching for him/her. Then, as one lamp lights another, the *guru* kindles the spiritual fire in the student. The two together make the Truth a living force. Therefore, in our tradition, the *guru* considers the disciple as the very form of *Bhagavati* and even worships him in the final initiation ceremony.

Thus, when you meditate, you must invite the *gurus* of the *mandala* to come and reside in you. Allow them to meditate in your body. Such surrender will make your progress easy.

229. GURUMAHARAJ

D: Babaji, tell us something about our great *guru*, your *guru*.

Babaji (closing his eyes in reverence and devotion)**:** Please don't address him merely as *guru*. You may call me whatever you like, but please address him only as *Gurumaharaj*.

How shall I describe the glory of that great one? You know, it is said that he was around 600 years old, but to me, he seemed like he was only 16, so tender and soft was his body, with hardly any hair covering it.

But, not until I had roamed the jungles hungry and thirsty, for three years, did he reveal himself to me. In the process, I met many rogues, charlatans and imposters. I also met well-meaning *sadhus* who told me that they were not my masters and assured me that I would find the master soon.

One day, as I lay burning with high fever, body aching with hunger and thirst, I saw a Presence standing in front of me. He offered his hand to me, but instead of holding on to it, I rushed for some water to quench my parched throat and he disappeared. How I wished that I had held on to him and not my thirst! My bodily needs were still far greater than the search for Truth. For another three years I roamed, searching the face that was carved in my heart.

Finally, I was told about a *siddha* who lived in a remote snow clad cave at Tunganath; a siddha who never spoke or ate or moved from his seat. He was quite inaccessible. The only way to reach him, was by placing a bag of grain outside his cave, as an offering. If you were lucky enough, your offering would be accepted and you would be granted an audience with him. I somehow managed to get a bag of grain from the villagers, to make my offering. Luckily for me, I was called in.

As I stepped into the cave, I saw only light and out of it slowly emerged this naked ascetic, luminous and peaceful, silent and motionless. It seemed like he had a body of light.

And do you know what my first great *sadhana* was? I was assigned the task of grazing cows. Can you imagine, a proud and successful businessman like me, was given a menial task of grazing cows? Can you imagine the battering my ego took? Here I was, looking forward to challenging penances and waiting to show my spiritual mettle. O, what a let down this tame and tedious chore of grazing cows was! I had heard of many types of *sadhanas,* but this one really puzzled me. Had I given up my lucrative career for this? Was this *sadhana* commensurate with my intelligence? What sense of accomplishment could I get from grazing cows?

Little did I realise, that my ego was hoping for an impressive *sadhana*. However, grazing cows was not as easy as it seemed. In the steep mountains, there was always a fear of the cattle falling off the cliff. Throughout the day, I would guard the cattle, running here and there in tension and fear. What a life and what a *sadhana!* In return, all I got was a handful of soaked chick peas for sustenance. Shattered lay my image of sitting at the feet of a benign master and listening to lofty Truths!

I did this duty for, what seemed like a long time, till one day, I just gave up. Let what is to happen, happen, I thought. Let the cows fall off or die; I am fed up. However, in the evening, the cows came back on their own. I learnt a vital lesson - you 'do' nothing, only *Bhagavati* 'does'. I also learnt that for a *sadhaka*, everything is a *sadhana* and whatever other mundane work or duties he may do, his *spiritual sadhana* must not stop. Not that

I had yet fully surrendered. One day, I started grumbling and abusing *Gurumaharaj*. I was immediately called to his cave.

D: How did he find that out? Who told him about it?

Babaji: Do you think he needed to be told anything? He divined our every thought and never instructed us in audible language. All his instructions were heard here, in the heart. He was a great master. He did not need to speak and go yakety yak like me.

D: Then what happened?

Babaji: *Gurumaharaj* called me in and struck me on the head, with his stick. That is all. I started bleeding profusely. 'Let the impure blood flow out', *Gurumaharaj* said, with a tone of finality. His authority was unimpeachable and his actions indebatable. He then touched the wound. The bleeding stopped immediately and the wound healed completely! The co-disciples thought I was blessed to get this thrashing from the master! Of course, I still had my doubts. After this, I was sent to a cave to meditate.

D: So he was very strict is it, and not loving and lenient like you?

Babaji: He was all love, but very strict. Tell me, what except pure love can motivate a master? What has he to gain from you, what but your good can there be in his heart? But yes, his was a silent love, and his manner was strict. (laughing) Because of my experiences with him, I had decided, that I would never be so strict with my disciples.

D: How did he show his displeasure with you?

Babaji: O, one look was enough. I could never argue with him as you people do with me. Once, he asked me to take a jar of milk to a co-disciple who was doing *sadhana*. This was a part of the *seva* that every *sadhaka* had to do in the *gurukula*. That day there was a landslide and the mountains were still shaking. I refused to go with the milk, arguing that, if something were to happen to me, I would die without finding the Truth.

Gurumaharaj gave me one look and I turned around and started to go. Suddenly the landslide was arrested and when I turned around, what do I see? *Gurumaharaj* stood with his hand raised, forbidding the mountain to move. That day I saw the power of that great master and love too. From then on, I learnt not to challenge him in any way or question his actions or motives.

D: How many disciples like you, were there in the *gurukulam*?

Babaji: Only a few, but they were all far more advanced than I was.

D: Ok, then what happened?

Babaji: I was sent to meditate in a cave. Everyday a jar of milk was sent to me. The mouth of the cave was sealed and I was confined in it.

D: For how long?

Babaji: For six months. All instructions given by *Gurumaharaj* were heard here, in my heart. One day he sucked my tongue and all impurities were removed. Soon I was given my final initiation *(diksha)* - the *sanyasa diksha*. On that day, he bathed me, worshipped me and removed my sacred thread.

D: Why?

Babaji: Because a *sanyasi* has no caste. I was asked to hang that sacred thread on a tree. Then he touched my head and ... (Babaji closed his eyes in bliss). Then I was asked to leave the *ashram*. I pleaded to be allowed to live with him and serve him.'Having found you now, I do not wish to lose you', I said. He would hear nothing of it. 'Your work awaits you. You have to go', he said. But you know, the beauty is that I never feel that he's away from me. His Presence lives with me at all times, in my heart. I never miss him, because he is always there with me.

D: Babaji, do you have a picture of him?

Babaji: No. Many times I tried to capture him on film, but failed. But this *rudraksha mala* that I wear and the conch that he had given to me are treasured symbols of *Gurumaharaj*.

D: What was his name Babaji?

Babaji(sticking out his tongue)**:** Just as a high born woman does not refer to her husband by his first name, so also in our *sampradaya,* we are not supposed to take the name of the *guru*. Anyway, his name was Shri Svarupanandaji Saraswati.

D: So, was your final initiation the last time that you saw him?

Babaji: No. I saw him once more, at the time of his *mahasamadhi*. That was on 14th April 1992. All the disciples were asked to be present on that day.

D: How did he inform you of this event?

Babaji(Smiling)**:** Oh, the *gurus* have their own methods of communication. That day, the weather was particularly bad. It was snowing and I was ill equipped for the journey. In the last lap of the journey, I was totally fagged out, when a tall, fair, young man offered to lead me on. I am sure it was a messenger of *Gurumaharaj*. He carried me all the way on his shoulders. The other disciples, who were accomplished *siddhas,* had come by the use of their super-natural powers. My co-disciples are senior to me in age and spiritual accomplishment. Some of them are 190 years old, some even more!

On that day, *Gurumaharaj* was seated there ready, to take leave and give up his body. As per tradition, he was to select a successor. All of us stood before him when, looking in my direction, he said, "come here." I looked back to see who he was calling, for surely it could not be me! I was not only the youngest, but also the least advanced spiritually.

Once again, *Gurumaharaj* pointed at me. I took a step forward and he put his *rudrakshamala* around my neck. And before I knew it, all my co-disciples, without a moment's hesitation, fell at my feet. (Babaji with tears in his eyes) Such humility! Here I was, a 'nobody' and I was being crowned the king!

Soon *Gurumaharaj* took his *mahasamadhi*. A ray of light emerged from his right toe and reached the top of his head, forming an *'aum'* in his body. The next moment, there lay a

heap of ashes at the spot where *Gurumaharaj* sat.
Then on, I was given the power to initiate aspirants on this path. At any given time, only one person can be the *guru* of a *gurumandala.* That responsibility, has now fallen on my shoulders. However, I am only an instrument of that divine master. A fool like me is worshipped because of his light. I am nothing. (Closing his eyes and lost in the bliss of chanting *'shri gurave namah shri gurave namah, shri gurve namah shri gurave namah. Shri...'* sits in deep silence.)

230. THE SIGNIFICANCE OF LALITA PANCHARATNAM

॥ श्रीललिता पञ्चरत्नम् ॥

प्रातःस्मरामि ललितावदनारविन्दं ।
बिम्बाधरं पृथुलमौक्तिकशोभिनासम् ।
आकर्णदीर्घनयनं मणिकुण्डलाढ्यं
मन्दस्मितं मृगमदोज्ज्वलभालदेशम् ॥१॥

At dawn, I meditate on the smiling lotus face of Lalita, lips resembling the bimba fruit, nose effulgent with a big pearl, with long eyes extending upto the ears, that are adorned with precious eardrops, and forehead decorated with kasturi.

प्रातर्भजामि ललिताभुजकल्पवल्लीं
रक्ताङ्गुलीयलसदंगुलिपल्लवाढ्याम् ।
माणिक्यहेमवलयाङ्गदशोभमानां
पुन्ड्रेक्षुचापकुसुमेषुसृणीर्दधानाम् ॥२॥

At dawn, I worship the kalpaka-creeper (kalpa vriksha) like arms of Lalita, her tender leaf like fingers, luminous with rings set with precious stones, wearing gem-set bangles and the shoulder adornment 'angada', bearing the stripped sugar-cane bow, flower, arrows and mace.

प्रातर्नमामि ललिताचरणारविन्दं
भक्तेष्टदाननिरतं भवसिन्धुपोतम् ।
पद्मासनादिसुरनायकपूजनीयं
पद्माङ्कुश ध्वजसुदर्शनलाञ्छनाढ्यम् ॥३॥

At dawn, I salute the lotus feet of Lalita, fulfiller of the wishes of devotees, the propellor to cross the ocean of samsara, worthy of worship by Brahma and other gods, decorated by the streaks of lines in the form of lotus, trident, flag and chakra.

प्रातः स्तुवे परशिवां ललितां भवानीं
त्रय्यन्तवेद्यविभवां करुणानवद्याम् ।
विश्वस्य सृष्टिविलयस्थितिहेतुभूतां
विश्वेश्वरीं निगमवाङ्मनसातिदूराम् ॥४॥

At dawn, I sing the song of praise of the very auspicious Lalita, Bhavani, whose glory is to be known through the Upanishads, who is full of compassion, who is the prime cause of creation, protection and destruction of the universe, who is the Goddess of the universe, who is beyond the comprehension of scriptures, speech and mind.

प्रातर्वदामि ललिते तव पुण्यनाम
कामेश्वरीति कमलेति महेश्वरीति ।
श्रीशांभवीति जगतां जननी परेति
वाग्देवतेति वचसा त्रिपुरेश्वरीति ॥५॥

O Lalita, at dawn I repeat your good names: Kameshvari (the goddess of desire), Kamala (the one who holds a lotus), Maheshvari (The Goddess of all goddesses), Shambhavi (the consort of Shambhu),

Jagatam janani (the mother of the universe), Vaak devata (the presiding deity of speech) Para (and beyond), Tripureshvari (the goddess of the three cities).

यः श्लोकपञ्चकमिदं ललिताम्बिकायाः
सौभाग्यदं सुललितं पठति प्रभाते ।
तस्मै ददाति ललिता झटिति प्रसन्ना
विद्यां श्रियं विपुलसौख्यमनन्तकीर्तिम् ॥६॥

He who reads at dawn, these five melodious and glorious verses in praise of Lalita is bestowed ere long, with the presence of Lalita, knowledge, happiness/bliss, wealth and infinite fame.

In the early hours of the morning, Babaji would wake up and sitting in *padmasana*, would begin his day, by reciting the *Lalita Pancharatnam,* written by *Bhagvan Shri Shankaracharya*. This was a daily ritual.
D: Babaji, what is the meaning of this *stotra*?
Babaji: 'O mind, on waking up in the morning, remember the goddess Lalita in her beautiful form. Remember her lotus like face, her lips like the red *bimba* fruit and the priceless pearl that adorns her nose. She has long eyes that seem to extend to her ears and her ears are adorned with *kundalas* made of precious stones.' Do you understand the significance of large eyes that stretch to the ears?

D: No Babaji.
Babaji: It means Her eyes can hear and Her ears can see.
D: How so Babaji?
Babaji: All senses are actually one. When you reach a state of Oneness, the senses can take on each other's roles. They become heightened and even go beyond their natural states and limitations. As Consciousness expands, you can see and hear things happening in times and places far removed from you. Not only that, but by listening you can see the corresponding images and by seeing, you can hear the corresponding sounds. When you become like *Bhagavati, ekatma* and *ekarasa,* you will also experience these things. Remember these Gods and Goddesses are forms of your own Consciousness.
D: So should this prayer be recited every morning?
Babaji: Morning is only an analogy for awakening. Whenever you are in an awakened state, it is morning, whenever you are in an awakened state remember only Her, for She, is the form of that awakened state. Try to be in that state always. That is the gist of this prayer.
D: And the next stanza Babaji?
(Babaji was lost in deep meditation.Later, even he would not remember the deeper meanings of the *stotra* that he had shared in that state! Learning with Babaji had no beginning and no end, was neither complete nor incomplete. In a sense, one even learnt to let go of the need to learn 'fully' and 'completely'; the need to accomplish.)

231. THE LIGHT OF TRUTH WILL ALWAYS GLOW

Babaji : You know, once I told *Gurumaharaj* that, the world is in need of people who will work to improve its condition. So,what good can be achieved by his living incognito, in this remote cave? He said, 'The sun is millions of miles away from the earth, but does it not reach the remotest corners of the earth?' The light of Truth, wherever it is, will always glow.

232. BABAJI, FROM WHERE ARE YOU?

Visitor: Babaji, are you from Punjab?
Babaji: This body is from Punjab.

233. BABAJI, WAS IT RIGHT OF YOU TO TAKE SANYASA?

D: Babaji, To find God, you left your wife and six young children to find God. Was that right? Did you not feel a sense of duty towards them?
Babaji: There is no duty higher than the duty to find God or find your Self. When an intense urge to find that arises in you, all other urges and duties fall away. If you feel divided, between your worldly duties and a duty to your Self; it means that the urge to find God is not strong enough and you are not ready to renounce duty. You cannot rationalise these actions. On the other hand, once you are free and find God, you realise that you do not owe anything to anybody. In the grandeur of that Truth, all human duty and action seems so puny. When there is no 'me' and 'mine', what duty can there be? You serve everyone and every act is an act of Love, and not duty.
As for my family, I am deeply grateful to my wife, for allowing me to go and pursue my *sadhana*. In my absence, she raised six fine children, single-handedly. Her *sadhana* is far greater than mine. Above all, *Bhagvati* looked after all of them. As *Shri Krishna* says in the *Gita*, "I do the works of those who come to Me."
D: So then, can we find God without leaving home and hearth?
Babaji: O! I was a mad man. You do not have to imitate my madness. What happened to me, and the inner state that made me take the decisions I did, will not enter you simply by imitating my actions. Besides, I went in search of a *guru*. You have already found yours.
Even after having realised the Truth, some cannot come to terms with the world and need to leave it behind. Others may

live in the world, untouched by it. *Gurumaharaj* also married, but he lived as a householder only for a few days! In any case, the inner state of a realised soul is the same.

234. TRUTH IS PRICELESS

D: Babaji, in finding the Truth, you lost many things. You gave up family, relationships, wealth ... any regrets?

Babaji: None at all. All my so-called sacrifices are worth a fistful of sand, compared to the Glorious Truth that I have experienced.

235. ROBES OF FIRE

Often, when Babaji would be standing at the station or when he would doze off on the platform while waiting for someone; strangers and commuters would give him *bhiksha,* unasked. He would then come home and gleam – 'See how much money I collected today at the station. I did not beg, they just offered it while I was asleep.'

D(joking)**:** Babaji, your attire with orange robes and *rudraksha malas* is cheap and easy. With a little bit of investment, you are ready to play your role of a Babaji.

Babaji: *Beta,* these orange robes bring with them a tremendous responsibility. Orange is the colour of fire and hence of purity and non-attachment (*vairagya*). Only he, in whom the impurities are destroyed, can qualify to wear them.

D: Babaji, how did you start wearing them?

Babaji: I used to wear white clothes. One day a disciple said, 'you will look good in orange robes, let me dye your clothes.' And that's how I started wearing orange clothes. What you wear, is anyway hardly of any importance.

D: Babaji, why do you not wear stitched *kurtas* like some *sadhus*?

Babaji: A *sanyasi* is supposed to wear unstitched cloth, a cloth in which there will be no knots. The unstitched garment, free of knots, is a symbol of the unobstructed psychological state of a *sanyasi.*

236. LEARNING SACRED VERSES

Babaji could recite the *Bhagavad Geeta* at the age of four.
Babaji: This learning of sacred *stotras* and *pathas,* is a very good discipline. These may not be understood and comprehended in childhood but when you mature, they come back to you and acquire a deep meaning. Thus, the learning of *subhashitas* and *stotras* should be an important part of the education of children.

237. THE IMPORTANCE OF SPEAKING THE TRUTH

Babaji would often narrate, how his father thrashed him for lying. He would argue with his father thus, 'Why should I speak the truth, if it only invites beatings and humiliation?' Remembering this childhood incident, he would explain to us –
Babaji: I realised only much later, that one speaks the Truth so that one's own *sattva* is not destroyed and not to conform to the norms of 'right' and 'wrong', set by society. Any action that produces divisiveness in you should be avoided, because divisiveness takes away the integration of our personality. Truth is Whole and to find it, you must remain whole. Never do that which you feel is wrong. Feelings of guilt, lying, rigid 'dos' and 'don'ts' and any form of disharmony between speech, thought and action, takes away the wholeness in you and divides you. The price you pay is lack of integration and spontaneity.

238. I CAN'T KILL

At the *ashram,* learning would happen at night. To spend a night at the *ashram,* in solitude, with Babaji, was the greatest good fortune that a disciple could hope for. Unusual stories, experiences and events of his life would unfold, transporting one into another world.

Often Babaji, in a state of deep inward mood, would say many things that were difficult to understand. Later he would not remember them because, he would say, they arose from another level of Consciousness. On one such occasion, he was revealing the secret of the martial arts wherein, by pressing certain points in the body or through inconspicuous blows, an air bubble would be created in the blood stream. This would expand and burst, as it reached the heart, thus killing a person.

D: Babaji, where did you learn all this?

Babaji: I was trained in killing. One day, my teacher asked me to kill someone and I said, 'I am sorry I can't do that', and gave up the training. But it has taught me the secrets of the body and what a great instrument it is.

239. DON'T EMULATE THESE HABITS OF MINE

D: Babaji, why do you smoke?

Babaji: When I go into deeply meditative states, it becomes difficult for me to maintain outer consciousness. Smoking keeps me in the outer consciousness or helps me to get back to it. But do not emulate my habits. It is not always advisable to do what the *guru* does. Do what he asks you to do, because that will be good for you. You must remember that whatever I ask you to do, will always be for your good.

240. BABAJI'S BEARD

Babaji had a flowing silvery beard. Disciples would playfully caress it. It had a warmth that was extremely soothing.

Babaji: You know, if you take a hair from my beard and put it in a book, then you will be able to remember the contents of that book easily.

D (joking)**:** So the next time we, or our children need to memorise a book, we will simply start plucking your beard.

Babaji (sternly)**:** This is not a joke. And please do not make fun of my body. This body belongs to *Gurumaharaj*. It is most sacred.

241. BABAJI'S METHOD

D: Babaji, what can your path be called? I find that it is a combination of meditative techniques, breathing techniques, worship of a personal god or *ishta devata* alongside, living spirituality. This seems to include the practice of awareness or conscious doing, in day to day life, while cleansing of the psyche of all preferences, inhibitions and conditionings. Am I right Babaji?
Babaji: I take, from different systems and masters, whatever I feel will help the student. I amalgamate many techniques. As such, *Gurumaharaj* never taught me any systems or techniques.
D(laughing): Ah! Babaji, you are the Padma Subramaniyam of spirituality.
Babaji: Who is she?
D: She is a great classical Indian dancer who has created a syncretic form of Indian dance by amalgamating all the classical dance styles.
Babaji: Ok, so you can call me the Padma Subramaniyam of spirituality. You can call me whatever you like. It does not bother me. This is my form of *Shaktiyoga.*You can even call it *Rajayoga*.

242. SHAKTIYOGA

D: Babaji,why is your *ashram* called *Shaktiyogashrama*? What is *Shaktiyoga*?
Babaji: The purpose of human birth is to expand Consciousness, to raise potential energies lying coiled up at the base of the spine, in the *muladharachakra*. This energy or *Kundalinishakti,* which is in the form of a serpent, coiled three and a half times, has to rise to meet her beloved *Shiva,* in the *sahasrara padma,* or the center of Consciousness, at the top of

the head, in the form of a thousand petalled lotus.

There are six such major *chakras* or centers of Consciousness inside the spine, on a *nadi* or energy channel called the *sushumna*. Along the path, this *shakti,* meets many obstructions, as many knots have to be broken. These are the *granthis* or knots that the *Lalita Sahasranama* talks of. These knots are the obstacles, in the form of your inhibitions and ignorance *(avidya),* that have to be removed by *sadhana.*

This *sadhana* includes, all *shastra* based or scientific techniques of postures, breathing and meditation, forms of initiation or *diksha* and of course, all techniques of awareness building; because unbroken awareness is the end of all *sadhana.*

It also includes methods that a *guru* spontaneously uses, to awaken a student. These can be in the form of talks or simple potent questions that create in the student, at that very moment, a state of *satori* or awakening, This method is spontaneous, interactive and unique to every individual *guru;* it cannot be a part of any system. It arises from the *guru's* spontaneous assessment, of the disciple's state of consciousness, at that moment and his readiness to grasp the truth. There is nothing mechanical or pre-determined about these methods. Thus, they offer, an ever-present opportunity to the disciple, to grow and jump out of his mundane consciousness. *Shaktiyoga* consists of all those methods that can take a disciple from the state of being a *jiva,* to that of being *Shiva.*

243. COSMIC MIND

D: Babaji, how do you know so much, on so many varied topics such as *ayurveda*, magic, palmistry etc.?

Babaji: All knowledge comes from the cosmic mind. You must learn to tune into that; then you can understand any subject.

244. RUN WITHIN

Once, there was an earthquake. All the disciples ran out of

the cottage, when it started quaking. Only Babaji remained seated, in deep meditation. After the earthquake subsided, the disciples came back and asked –

D: Babaji, Why did you also not run?

Babaji: I too ran, but not outside. I ran inside, inside my Self.

245. CAN A BABAJI EAT ICE CREAM ?

Babaji: Would you like to eat some ice cream?

D(surprised): Do you eat ice-cream?

Babaji: Yes, why? Can't a Babaji eat ice cream? It is the inner state of a Babaji that is important. Don't judge a Babaji by external acts.

246. THE DEMANDING TONGUE

Babaji: Please put some more sugar in my tea. (On second thoughts) No, forget about it. See how this tongue starts demanding!

(Talking to his tongue) My dear one, you seem to have forgotten days spent in the jungle, without a drop of tea! In my *sadhana* days, when I was studying the *vedas* and *upanishads* in solitude, I would hang a piece of bread from a wire, promising myself, that if a single thought of food crossed my mind, I would not eat it. I have spent months living off the peels of bananas and today, this tongue wants more sugar. It is true that a *sadhu* should live alone, in austerity and simplicity.

247. THE MIND IS NOT FOR PRESERVATION

It was lunchtime. A disciple had cooked a meal for Babaji, when he showed a desire to visit his family, and have lunch there. But on second thoughts, Babaji started to serve himself the meal at hand.

D: Babaji, your mind feels like going to your home, doesn't it?

Babaji: So? Do I have to make an *'achar'* (pickle or preserve) of this mind ? Do I have to preserve this mind – its desires and wishes?

248. BABAJI TO BE JAILED

Once, Babaji was caught traveling ticket-less because he was engrossed in talking and forgot to buy a ticket.

TC: Babaji, this is a serious offence and you can be jailed for this.

Babaji: My son, it was not intentional, but if you must jail me, go ahead. I am sure only human beings live there.

249. 'I' REMAIN THE SAME

D: Babaji, *ab apko tond aa gayi* – now a pot belly has developed on you.

Babaji: Let whatever has to come, come; and whatever has to go, go; 'I' remain the same.

250. A CURE FOR POTBELLY

Babaji would share with us many instances, of how, he would converse with *Devi,* and she would give him invaluable guidance. Once, he was saying his morning prayers, when suddenly, *Devi* started laughing at him.

He asked her, "Why are you laughing at me?"

She said, "Look at your pot belly, you are putting on weight!"

Babaji asked, "So what should I do?"

She said, "Every morning, as soon as you get up, before you eat anything, recite the *Lalita Sahasranama."*

D: So, do you do that Babaji?

Babaji: Of course, how can I disobey Her?

251. FOOD IS BHAGAVATI

In his last days, when he was unwell, instead of light food that his delicate health demanded, gram pulse was cooked by mistake, at the *ashram.*

D: Babaji, this is not good for you. Let me make a light soup for you.

Babaji: Nothing is 'bad.' Food is *Bhagavati.* It cannot harm me. Let me eat it.

252. BABAJI AVOIDED DOCTORS

Babaji rarely went to a doctor. He always maintained – 'It is my body, how can someone else understand it?' Once, a poisonous snake bit him. He tied the infected part while reciting a *mantra.* In a few days, he was alright.

253. THAT'S ALL I KNOW

Babaji was humming away an item number from a Hindi film – *'tu cheej badi hai mast mast* - you are an intoxicating thing (woman)!'

D (amused and scandalised)**:** Babaji, what are you singing? This is a sensuous number, that a hero is singing to his heroine in a commercial Hindi film.

Babaji: So what? I am also singing it to my heroine, *Bhagavati Devi.*

D (laughing)**:** Babaji, you even sing these sensuous numbers like *bhajans.*

Babaji: That's all I know.

254. BABAJI'S DANCE

D: Babaji, what is this dance that you are doing?

Babaji: It has no name. It is my dance of joy!

255. PLEASE GIVE ME DIKSHA

D: Babaji, please give me *diksha* (initiation).

Babaji: *Arre,* that is not in my hands. They, the *gurus,* initiate. I am only an instrument. Ask them for the initiation.

256. NONE BUT THE 'I'

Babaji was leaving for the Himalayas -

D: Babaji, are you going alone?

Babaji: You know what is the meaning of 'alone'? It means, 'All One,' 'whole.' Yes, I am always going 'alone.' The disciple gives him a huge hamper of food.

Babaji: O my god, so much food?
D: Yes, so that you have enough for yourself, after you have distributed it to 'others'.
Babaji: Others? There are no others. There is only I, and none other. I pervade everything – *'sirf mai hi mai hoon, doosra koi hai hi nahin.'*

257. I AM SORRY BABAJI

D(arriving late for a visit)**:** I am so sorry Babaji, but...
Babaji: Don't be sorry. There should be no place for sorrow in life.

258. FAVOURITE DISCIPLES

D: Babaji, do you have favourites among your disciples?
Babaji: No, none. I am interested in everyone's well being. Yet, disciples are at different levels, their needs are different and accordingly time has to be spent with them. But mark my words, all those who come in contact with me, will definitely have the grace of *Bhagavati.*

259. GURUSEVA

D: Babaji, today I am going to feed you two or three different kinds of sweets.
Babaji (giggling)**:** O, please spare me that.
D (laughing)**:** No, I want to do *guruseva*. Babaji, shall I tell you a joke?
Babaji: Sure.
D: Once, a *sadhu* was bathing. A man came and started pouring, jug after jug of cold water on him.
The *sadhu* said 'O, stop it, I am freezing.'
The man said, 'No, no. I want to do *seva.* The *shastras* say that, it is good to do *guruseva!'*
Babaji: (rolling with laughter and then in a more serious tone) Every disciple wants to do *guruseva,* but according to his own

whims and fancies and likes and dislikes. *Guruseva* means, to do what the *guru* wants you to do, and not, doing whatever you feel like doing, for the *guru*.

260. THAT'S HOW I LEARNT TO MEDITATE

Referring to the severe penance, that *Gurumaharaj* had ordained him to do –

Babaji: Once, I told *Gurumaharaj* that I could not enter the meditative state. He reprimanded, 'How dare you not?'. So saying, he soaked a blanket in the icy waters of the Himalayan rivers, flung it on me and said, 'Now don't get up till the heat produced by meditation, dries this completely'. That is how I learnt to meditate!

261. A STORY OF AN AGHORA BABA

Babaji: Once, a friend and I, were walking in the jungle. We came across an *aghori baba,* who started throwing stones at us, as soon as he saw us. My friend fled in fear, but I continued to walk towards him. He kept on hurling the stones, though not a single one hit me, since it was aimed to only pass close to my body. As I neared him, he threw a piece of flesh that he was eating and commanded – 'eat it.' I realised that this is no ordinary person. Without flinching, I took the flesh and started eating it. It was absolutely sweet!

In some time, I came back to my friend and narrated the entire incident to him. He said, 'Lets go back and meet him.' We retraced our steps and reached the spot where he was sitting. Now nobody was there. Neither the stones, nor the pieces of flesh that he had thrown at us, were to be found. I asked my friend, 'Why did you run away? You have missed the opportunity to be blessed by a *siddha*. You were not destined to have his *prasada*.'

D: But Babaji, how does one know that this is an opportunity and not a trick being played by a rogue?

Babaji: These incidents test your innate purity. The cerebral mind cannot be used here, to rationally gauge a situation. If you act from past experience, you will only be misled. But remember, Grace will always descend like this – unannounced. You cannot be trained to receive grace.

262. A STORY FROM BABAJI'S SADHANA DAYS

Babaji never tried to conceal the mistakes he had made as a *sadhaka*. He was never afraid, that it would violate his image as a *guru*. This lack of guile, this humility and acceptance of his human weaknesses in fact, also encouraged us to be completely frank and open about our shortcomings.

Babaji: You know, once during the *sadhana* period, *Gurumaharaj* asked me to go and collect *bhiksha*. A young girl gave me some *bhiksha* and while talking to her, I offered to read her palm, and on that pretext, held it in my hand. When I returned to the *ashram*, *Gurumaharaj*, who divined every single act and thought of ours said, 'So, you might as well have gone all the way in making physical contact. Anyway, mentally you had. So what difference would the physical act have made!'

263. THE FINAL INITIATION

Referring to his final initiation, he reminiscenced how, *Gurumaharaj* bathed him in milk, performed on him, all the *pujas* that one would, on a deity, worshipping him, with the *shodashopacara* or sixteen rituals. *Gurumaharaj* then, removed his sacred thread, hung it on a tree, explaining, 'from today, you are a *sanyasi;* and a *sanyasi* has no *kula* or caste'. Then, he asked me to leave.

Babaji: How can I leave, I have still not attained.

Gurumaharaj: My dear, as soon as a woman conceives, she does not deliver a child, she has to wait for 9 months. After some time, *purna jnana* or Total Knowledge will be bestowed on you.

Babaji: Thus, for sometime, I roamed the jungles, naked

and free. One day, I poured a pot of hot water on my body and nothing happened. Another time, when some people were thirsty and could not find any water to drink, I simply dug the ground, and a spring of water emerged. These were all proofs, of the tremendous *yoga shakti* or spiritual powers that, *Gurumaharaj* had bestowed on me. In a sense, they were also a test of my character. If I would have given in to the temptation of misusing those *siddhis*, I would have never matured spiritually.

264. WHAT IS IN A NAME ?

D: Babaji, how come you do not have the typical name that all *sanyasis* have – the *dasha nama* or ten titles like *giri, ananda, saraswati* etc.?

Babaji: Oh yes, my *sanyasa* name is *Suprabuddhananda*. However, when *Gurumaharaj* whispered it in my ears, I laughed and said Super *Buddha*! Then I asked him why I needed another name – what is wrong with my original name? As was his style, Gurumaharaj said nothing. That is how I decided to retain my original name.

265. THE GODDESS IS IN ALL WOMEN

Babaji 'saw' the Goddess in all women and was often misunderstood for that. Often, in a trance like state, he would recite the appropriate name of the Goddess, when he would see a lady. In ecstacy, he would variously address her as, *'subhru'* – one with a beautiful brow, *'nilachikura'* – one with the dark tresses, *'sumukhi'* - one with a beautiful face. Once, on seeing the *mangala sutra* dangling from a lady disciple's neck, he burst forth, *'kamesha baddha mangalya sutra shobhita kandhara* - the *mangala sutra* tied by *kamesha shiva,* adorns her neck.' Many such names of the Goddess, describing her beautiful form, would spontaneously burst forth from his lips, when he saw beauty in anyone.

Distinctions between real life and higher truths often blurred, as he thus responded. The sacred beauty of nature revealed itself and we saw ourselves as parts of that divine beauty and play. In fact, once, when he complimented a disciple on her beautiful eyes and when she, in pride, she started enjoying the compliment, he said, 'What are you feeling so proud of? Have you done anything to create those beautiful eyes? I am simply admiring the beautiful artisan that Nature is. Remember, this body is a gift given by Nature, it is not yours. You will have to return it to Nature.'

266. SHUN COMMERCIALISATION

Babaji disapproved of the urban mind set, that spent carelessly and indiscriminately. He felt that mindless buying, without assessing the value received against the price, can also corrupt the seller, while sowing the seeds of greed.

On the trek in the Himalayas,he took the disciples to some of the most beautiful yet remote places, that had no tourist trappings. At one such place called Madmaheshwar, there was no habitation, except for a shrine (one of the PanchKedar shrines) and a *dharmashala* (guest house for pilgrims). The disciples spent three days there. This, being right in the middle of the *yatra,* and the disciples were by now, reconciled to simple, frugal meals. All parameters of breakfast, lunch and dinner, had also been set aside by then. All concepts of, 'balanced meal', 'full meal' etc. were also layed to rest. A simple, hot meal, at any time of the day, was a great luxury. For the soft, city-bred disciples, any one who provided this luxury, was god.

At Madmaheshvar, a small eating-house, gave simple but hot food and good service too. While leaving the place, one of the disciples, warm with the food in his belly, in an expansive mood, settled the bill without negotiating and without taking consent from Babaji. Babaji soon found out - he had to! He seemed to have not three, but a hundred eyes and ears! His loud and clear response was, a resounding slap on the cheeks of this well placed, adult disciple! Later on he explained –

Babaji: Do not spoil people or fan their greed by raising monetary expectations. Today you can pay inflated rates, because of your urban yardsticks, but remember, that simple people and *sadhus* like me who frequent this place can ill afford high rates. You are making things difficult for those simple people. Once the minds of the hotel owners are corrupted and commercialisation attracts them, these places will lose their sanctity and become like urban resorts. I have brought you on this *yatra,* (pilgrimage) to understand simplicity and shed urban gloss.

267. A LESSON IN TOUGHNESS AND TENDERNESS !

On the Himalyan trek, Babaji relentlessly challenged our notions and especially our needs for creature comforts and security. No reservations were made on buses or trains, no hotels were booked in advance and no fixed itineraries were followed. For 35 days, we did not know, when and where our next meal would come from, where we would spend the night and under what conditions. We never lived in hotels. With an uncanny sense, Babaji would locate large rooms in which we would all settle with our simple beddings. At the end of the day, so exhausted were we from the trek, that we were grateful for a roof over our head and some space to rest our tired backs. Some times, we traveled by the most crowded of buses, irritated at the commotion and disorder. And there Babaji would be, laughing away and cracking jokes. The message was clear – 'discomforts are for the body but you are not this body, you are the carefree spirit. Let the spirit soar.' In fact, by the end of the trip, we were prepared for the worst and had stopped dreaming of comforts.

Once after a grueling trek of 20 kms, our aching feet were

longing for a bus ride. As luck would have it, we missed the last bus. Babaji tried to hire a vehicle, while we waited with baited breaths for the negotiation to come through. The deal was struck, and hearts from the age of 7 to 70 leapt with joy. We comfortably parked ourselves in the bus and started believing in the goodness of God, when suddenly Babaji said, "Get down all of you, this man wants to cheat us. We can't pay his exorbitant rates." Without a murmur, we got down and in spite of the fatigue, hunger and darkness, walked the remaining 8 kms!

We wonder – can we do this again, without his high energy and unbending moral courage? Maybe not. But it has certainly taken away our fear of physical discomfort, giving us a toughness that is so essential to live spiritual values, for, soft bodies, can only house weak minds. Here were lessons taught, that mere recitation of *rama-nama* or discussion of philosophies, would never have achieved. This was hands-on spirituality. And how can one not respond when, after this tiring walk, just as we were ready to collapse out of hunger, Babaji again roamed the village to get some food for us, requesting shop keepers to spare whatever they could for his hungry children. What a lesson this was in toughness and tenderness!

268. BABAJI PLAYS NURSE

Babaji could be the most caring and affectionate nurse when one fell ill. Of course, the only medication he believed in was the *mantra* and the touch.

Once, a disciple was down with flu. Babaji offered to make clear soup for her. He asked the disciple's mother to bring out all the required vegetables. Meticulously and with total involvement, he started cutting the vegetables. Embarrassed, the mother offered to do the cutting and chopping.

Babaji: Do you think I am simply chopping and cutting the vegetables? I am empowering them with *mantras* from the *Lalitasahasranama*. See how she recovers once she drinks this soup.

269. ALL JIVAS WANT REST AND EASE

Once, Babaji was traveling in a jeep to the *ashram*. On the way, a dog was easing himself on the road. Babaji immediately asked the disciple who was driving the car, to stop until the animal had finished his job. The disciple was surprised and asked Babaji why he bothered to do that.

Babaji: If you were easing yourself and someone were to disturb you or scare you away, how would you feel? All *jivas* or souls want rest and ease.

270. A BABAJI MAY NOT TOUCH EVERYONE

D: Babaji, that man I introduced you to yesterday, did not take to you at all. I am unable to understand, how can you not touch someone?

Babaji (Laughing)**:** Ah, there you go flattering me again. (Becoming serious) Have you read that name of *Bhagavati* – '*pashulokabhayankari* – She is frightening and repulsive to the *pashus,* or those with animal tendencies.' Well, those who are insensitive, lacking in purity and lacking a sense of Truth, are actually frightened and threatened, by those who have it.

D: Babaji, do you not feel offended if you are misunderstood?

Babaji: Not at all. What matters to me is that, I should not misunderstand others.

271. BABAJI, WHY SO FEW?

On reading the book of a famous god man, a disciple was impressed by the large following he had.

D: Babaji, why do only a few people come to you, while there are unending queues, to get a glimpse of some of these god men?

Babaji: A diamond hidden in the womb of the earth is not priced. When it is brought out, then it has a high price. The diamond that has been given by our *guru* is hidden, it is not obvious, hence people cannot recognise it. Therefore there is less traffic here. But, a diamond is a diamond, whether seen or not, whether recognised as such, or not.

272. NO WORK IS BIG AND SMALL

Worker in the village: Babaji, we are simple labourers and your disciples are well heeled, educated *saabs,* working in big companies. We feel self conscious in their presence.

Babaji: There is no big or small work. It is immaterial, whether the work undertaken is big or small, physical or mental. What matters is, with what devotion, intensity and dexterity, you do the work.

Babaji himself was a living example of a dispassionate, choiceless approach to work. We had seen him work with equal facility, at diverse tasks. Whether it was collecting funds, or buying and bargaining for building materials for the *ashram* work, Babaji did it with equal ease. Whether it was conceptualising the vision of the *ashram gurukul* or simply picking up the hammer and chisel to substitute for an absent worker. Or whether it was even plunging into work in the kitchen after a full day's official work; Babaji displayed a choiceless and joyous involvement in whatever he did.

A lady disciple would joke, 'Babaji, now you are like a full-fledged, working woman!'

Again, he could completely drop all tasks, to sit in *dhyana,* lost to all external consciousness, swimming in bliss.

273. TEACHER MUST BE LIKE A SCULPTOR

Babaji was once watching a classical dance class and suddenly he said to the teacher –

Babaji: You are a hopeless teacher. A dance teacher must be like a sculptor. Just as a sculptor physically pats and shapes the clay, you must also mould and pat into shape, the bodies of your students.

274. I WOULD RATHER KEEP MY BABAJI WAYS

D: Babaji, you seem very preoccupied today. What are you thinking about?

Babaji: Well, it is about the land, that we need to get for the *ashram*. The owner is playing hide and seek and I do not know, if he will eventually, give the land to us.

D: Babaji, there are ways and means of getting that work done. But, you will have to leave your 'Babaji ways', and do it as we *samsari* (worldly) people do it.

Babaji: No. I would rather keep my 'Babaji ways'. *Bhagvati* will do, what is best for us.

275. EVERYONE WANTS TO BE A GURU !

A disciple was giving big talks about *adhyatma* or spiritual truths, to other disciples.

Babaji: Until you have the *adhikara* or right to talk about these truths, either with the permission of the master, or on the strength of your own *yoga abhyasa,* do not start giving lengthy sermons. It will inflate your ego, make you hollow from within and reduce the love of God in you. A *sadhaka* must watch out for these enemies of self-growth. Whatever you talk, should be from your own first hand experience; not from books and hearsay. Truth has to be a living experience. The problem is that, everyone wants to be a *guru!*

276. SHARING PERSONAL EXPERIENCES OF TRUTH

Once, a well-known industrialist and educationist, invited Babaji to attend a meeting of great scholars. He immediately divined that the industrialist wanted to test him. Nevertheless, he went along.

In the gathering were great scholars, some of whom spoke only in *Sanskrit*. Babaji sat listening to the august gathering. Finally, the host asked him to say something. He simply asked the scholars, 'Can you tell me anything, that you have personally experienced, which is not from books and *shastras*? I have only my personal experiences of Truth, to share with you. I am not a scholar.' The host and his team of scholars were completely baffled and sat speechless. They wanted to 'impress' and 'be impressed' by Babaji, but he nipped it in the bud.

Babaji: People like to be impressed!

D: Why is that so Babaji?

Babaji: Because the ego wants to be in the possession of grand things and experiences.

277. HOW YOU LOOK AT THINGS

With Babaji, learning was always in real time, here and now. Some of us at the *ashram,* had gone on a day-long excursion, in the neighbouring hills. We departed before the break of dawn, caught a breathtaking glimpse of the sun rising over the distant mountains, were entertained by birdsong, and talked about the wild animals one can encounter in the thick *Sahyadri* bamboo forest.

It was way past midnight, when Babaji was off for a walk, and some of us joined him. It was an *amavashya* (moonless) night, and we walked and walked. Returning to the *ashram* after a few hours, Babaji asked all, how the day went. Many from the group, broke into a litany of complaints, of how hard the going had been, plodding uphill and downhill, getting pricked by thorns, with pesky flies and frightening jungle noises to contend with, besides fear of close encounters with wild creatures. In short, it was a sheer waste of time, cribbed some of the stressed out companions. What to Babaji, was a wonderful outing in the forest, turned out to be a stressful day and a night, full of fear, worry and apprehension, for the city slicker!

Babaji (laughing)**:** Stress, in a way, lies in your attitude and the way you look at things.

278. A LAZY DISCIPLE

Babaji's *ashram* had no electricity. A single kerosene lamp, served to light up the room. Being a stickler for conservation, Babaji was very particular that, the lamp be turned to a low flame for the night and be snuffed out, as soon as one woke up. He was also very careful, to place the lamp in such a way that, the kerosene fumes, were not directly inhaled. In this last ritual of the day, it was difficult to please Babaji and come up to his exacting standards! Sensing a disciple's laziness in this matter, he would often tell this little story –

Babaji: Once a *guru* asked his lazy disciple, to turn off the lamp for the night. The disciple said, 'Why don't you just turn the other way, so that the light does not enter your eyes'.

After some time, the cat started purring. The *guru* asked the disciple, to put the cat, out of the room. The disciple replied, 'Why don't you just cover your ears with a pillow and the noise will not bother you?'

Finally, the *guru* said, 'I am thirsty, can you get me a glass of water?' The disciple said, 'I have done two chores. Now you do the third one!'

279. IN THE KITCHEN WITH BABAJI

Cooking food with Babaji was always a great pleasure. He would casually reveal, the natural traits of *dals* and vegetables and they actually became living entities, with minds of their own.

- *Tur dal,* he would say, is very heavy and *tamasika.* A *sadhaka* should restrict its consumption, to the minimum. It is advisable for a *sadhaka,* to consume *mung dal.*
- The kernel of a cauliflower has great nutritional value; never throw it away.
- Green peas are tasty, but do not have much in terms of nutrition. Always use them only for taste and decoration.
- Raw onions are good for the eyes and roasted onions are good for the brain.

- Green chillies are not harmful; it is their seeds that cause damage. Always remember to de-seed them before using.
- The skin of an apple constipates; always peel an apple before eating it.
- A single almond, if rubbed and made into a paste, has far more nutritive value than a handful of almonds. Always soak and peel an almond before eating it.

And so on…

Above all, it was a great learning experience to watch, the complete absorption with which he did the smallest chore, whether of peeling the vegetables or washing the *dals.*

He made sure that, there was absolutely no wastage. The vegetable peels and water from washing the *dals,* was meticulously collected in a trough, in which the cattle were given their food. If one were to assist him in the cooking, he would be constantly giving instructions on washing the vegetables, deseeding the chillies and so on. The milk vessels, on being emptied, were further cleaned, by heating a little water in them to scrape off all the cream, that was obstinately stuck to the sides. In addition, if his hawk like eye caught one wasting anything, you had it! Jokingly, disciples would refer to him as, 'mother-in-law' because, of his constant nagging! And heavens forbid, if he found leftovers in our plate! Gently, yet sternly, he would say, 'And what crime has this poor vegetable committed that you are rejecting it? How would you feel, if someone did that to you?'

Often, he would prance around the kitchen in child like joy, opening cans and tins and talking to the contents therein. To him everything was living. He would say, 'Nothing is inanimate. It is your arrogance and self-importance that makes you think so. Why, have you not noticed that, if you leave a house and go away for a few years, the very dust eats it up? So now, can you call this dust inanimate?'

Sometimes, while the *dal* was cooking, he would sit with eyes closed, absorbed in deep meditation, letting out sounds of *'wah wah, wah wah'*, to express the deep, inner joy that he felt. A meal at the *ashram* would simply comprise of a simple *roti* and a vegetable, accompanied by a salad or potato chips (which he loved), and which he would fashionably refer to as a 'side dish'! Sometimes the meal would comprise of rice, *dal* and a vegetable. If on occasions, the entire combination was made, he would call it a feast. If a sweet dish were added to it, he would call it a banquet! We learnt simple and valuable food habits from these experiences. We also learnt how to cook and eat with love. Moreover, the love with which he fed us, would completely fulfill us.

Going to the *ashram,* was like going to one's mother's house. Babaji would spoil us silly while at the *ashram.* From his little Pandora's box of provisions, would emerge the best of *ghee* and honey, sweets and dry fruits, cheese and chocolates! In fact, Babaji always lived in a state of bounty and plenty. If we were to ask him, whether we should bring anything along, when we went to the *ashram,* he would say – *'Bhagvati ka bhandar hai. Jo lana chaho le aao. Kuch nahi laoge toh bhi chalega-* this is *Bhagavati's* treasury. Get what you feel like. Even if you get nothing, it is Ok.'

Lady disciples were pampered even more, as he sympathised with their lot and their struggle – physical, emotional and mental. He would allow them to rest, until late in the morning, while he would make hot breakfast for them. He would say, you know in Maharashtra, the *guru* is called *'guru mauli'* or *guru* mother.

Finally, the icing to the cake, were the nuggets of Truth that he shared with us in the kitchen. A single oil lamp would provide the light, while Babaji cooked and shared the truth with us. That single burning flame, heightened the ambience of deep introversion, that was needed to imbibe what he was imparting.

Once, Babaji was alone with a disciple at the *ashram*. Together, they were preparing food on the *chulha*.

D: Babaji, I understand all that you say and sincerely agree, that I must follow your advice and give priority to the *sadhana*. While I am at the *ashram*, I resolve to meditate regularly, but once I am back to the grind of city life and the routine of the *grihasti* (family life), the intensity waters down.

Babaji(pointing to the *chulha*)**:** See, when you are near the fireplace, you feel the warmth. The farther you go from it, the warmth decreases. So, you should keep coming to the fireplace(*guru*) repeatedly, until you catch the spark. Then, just as the wood put into the *chulha*, becomes fire itself, you too will become like me. Then, whether you are here or there, you will burn bright with the fire of Truth.

280. BATHING IN MILK AND HONEY AT THE ASHRAM

Milk and honey were available in abundance at the *ashram*. In fact, one of the enduring images we carry of Babaji at the *ashram*, is that of a *fakir* whose only job seemed to be that of reheating the milk every few hours. Due to the absence of a refrigerator, he would remove the cream that had gathered on top of the milk and once again reheat it, so that it would not get spoilt. The cream that would be preserved and fermented with a dash of curd, would yield ghee or clarified butter; the residual buttermilk would be eaten as an accompaniment to meals or else thirsty passers by and villagers, would be treated to it. It was amazing how he was never tired or got bored of these routine chores.

One could taste fresh milk, directly from the udders of a cow, at the *ashram*. Babaji would hear nothing about the harmful effects of milk or ghee. He would say, 'The ghee or milk, of cows that graze and are active through the day, can never be harmful. City cows, bred in the dairy, are made to simply sit and eat through out the day. They are thus slothful, and therefore their milk produces sloth. He also believed that, the milk from *desi* or indigenous cows, was much better, than the milk from Jersey cows.

Defending the medicinal powers of ghee, he would quote a Punjabi saying – 'Better one father, than a hundred uncles; and better one ghee, then a hundred medicines!' So saying, with squeals of satisfaction, he would help himself to tall glasses of milk. As he drank the milk, his thick moustache, would be soaked in the cream, from the milk. With firm strokes of his fingers, he would skillfully drain that cream into his mouth and lick it up with child-like joy. At such times, his Santa Claus like visage, looked no different from that of child *Krishna.*

Another pet topic was honey.

Big barrels of pure and processed honey were stored at the *ashram.* Babaji would obtain the honey from the tribals, seal it in big jars and then keep it under water for a year or two. This treatment he said, would take away the heat from the honey.

As disciples ate the honey, he would share information on the role of the bee and the queen bee, and the intelligence of the bee that collected the honey only from one type of tree. Thus, he would say, there are different types of honey and the medicinal property of the honey, depended on the tree, from which the honey was collected. Bitter honey, he would say, is a rarity, having the greatest medicinal value. Thus he would go on sharing insights and chattering joyfully.

We have forgotten a major part of those insights. What we do remember is that, milk and *ghee* were never so tasty, as at the *ashram.* Or, was it just his love, that made it so?

281. HORSING AROUND WITH BABAJI

Once, the disciples had gone to the *ashram,* to attend a meditation camp, organised by Babaji –

On such occasions, time-tables were rarely made; rarer still was the adherence to them. Programmes emerged spontaneously. On this particular occasion, after a concentrated session, discussing many subtle principles of *sadhana,* Babaji suddenly announced that, they should all play a game. Everyone, including Babaji, played the game of Pillar to Post!

Often, if he sensed that the disciples were tired, he would cancel a meditation session. He would say, 'When you are too hungry, tired, or depressed, what is the point in meditating?'

Yet, Babaji's spontaneity was not a form of indiscipline. He seemed to respond, more to the inner state of a student, making programmes accordingly.

Consider this situation – Once, in an '*aumkara sadhana*' camp, the disciples, taking advantage of Babaji's principle of 'spontaniety', were nonchalantly chatting over cups of tea, while Babaji waited in the meditation hall. Babaji sensed the indisciplined mood of the students. He was livid with anger and gave us a good piece of his mind! Baffled disciples, scurried to their seats, sheepishly getting into asana!

He would often caution – 'Do, what the *guru* asks you to do, and not what he does. What he asks you to do, is good for you; what he does, springs from his inner state of mind. How can you imitate his mere action, when you have not attained that state of mind?'

Once at *puja* time, he said playfully, 'Just wait, while I say 'Hi' to *Bhagavati.*' Then, immediately he turned around and said, 'Only I can do this huh, you don't try it!'

Till today, the disciples find it most difficult, to understand Babaji's principle of 'spontaniety'.

282. READING WITH BABAJI

Babaji would often read aloud to us, sharing inspiring,spiritual stories.

Babaji: Listen, listen to this wonderful story, on the powers of meditation and states of *samadhi*!

Once, the *Buddha* was seated in *dhyana.* A big boulder came hurtling down, from the mountain-top. However, before it reached the *Buddha,* it clashed against another rock and split into two, flying on either side of the Buddha. A small splinter however, flew from the boulder and pierced the foot of the Buddha and it started bleeding.

The *Buddha* got up from *dhyana* and told his disciples – did you get a lesson in *samyak samadhi* (the highest form of non-dualistic Conscious awareness) from this? Had I not been in a state of *dhyana,* the huge boulder from the mountain-top, would have surely ripped me apart. On the other hand, since my state of *dhyana* was incomplete, this splinter injured me. This wound, is a sign of that incomplete state.

Babaji (still reading): And listen to this touching story of humility –

The great *natha siddha* Gorakshanath, had heard a lot about the spiritual prowess of the mystic saint Kabir. To test him, Gorakshanath challenged saint Kabir to a debate. Fixing his trident at the mystic's door, he suggested, they both should sit on the spokes, that are on either extremes of the trident, while *Brahma* would sit in the centre, as referee.

Saint Kabir, in all humility, declined the offer, not considering himself on par, with the great Gorakshanatha. Being a weaver, he brought out a bundle of thread from his house and threw it in the air. With his great yogic powers, the thread stood erect in space. Saint Kabir then, invited Gorakshanath to sit on the upper end of the thread, while he sat at the lower end, in keeping, he felt, with his spiritual status.

Pleased with the saint's humility and awe struck at his great, spiritual progress, *mahayogi* Gorakshanath told saint Kabir, to ask for a boon. Saint Kabir asked for 1/20th of the '*garibi*' (humility) in the world. Gorakshanath was dumb struck at this unusual request. He approached the Gods, asking for their help. The Gods politely declined, because it was a quality, that they themselves did not possess in abundance!

283. SHOPPING WITH BABAJI

Babaji seemed to enjoy bargaining. What he wanted to buy was, immaterial; equally irrelevant, was the price quoted! His reaction was standard.

Babaji (to a shopkeeper)**:** My son, how much is this for? (On hearing the price) *arre*, you want to fleece a poor Babaji!

D (Laughing)**:** Babaji, are you ever satisfied with the price? Why do you always bargain?

Babaji (Laughing)**:** Well, most of the time, I have an intuitive idea of the price. To over pay for something is not generosity, but stupidity. It also encourages dishonesty, because if once, the shopkeeper succeeds in over pricing, he will be tempted to make it a habit. Don't spoil people.However, the real reason is that, it gives me an opportunity to share my love, to connect with people, to understand their needs and problems. Those who reduce the price, do not suffer a loss; they gain blessings. The blessings of a Babaji are invaluable.

D: Babaji, are blessings of such importance?

Babaji: Of course. They are the real fruits of your good *karma.* (While talking, we moved to another shop.)

Babaji: My son, what is the price of this?

Shop keeper: *Arre* Babaji, you can have it for free.

Babaji: God bless you my child, but you know, I have a lot of money. And so saying, he paid the legitimate price!

284. MONEY IS NOTHING. LOVE IS EVERYTHING

Babaji often amazed one, with his lack of guile and immense sense of goodwill and brotherhood. Once, we were returning from the *ashram* and were already running late for the bus. Quickly, he stopped at the Lonavla market and told one of the shopkeepers. '*Arre beta,* I have to go to Mumbai, just give me

Rs.200 for travel.' Without batting an eyelid, the shopkeeper reached his kitty and handed over the required sum of money. The disciple stared in disbelief.
Babaji: *Arre beta,* money is nothing. Love is everything.

285. BHIKSHA FOR SHIVRATRI

Babaji: Please help me collect *bhiksha* for *Shivratri.*
D: And how should one do that?
Babaji: Ask everyone you know, to contribute in whatsoever measure they can.
D (after a few days, handing over the *bhiksha* book to Babaji): Here Babaji, I have collected some *bhiksha* for *Shivratri.*
(Babaji comes to know, that the disciple has not asked for *bhiksha,* but instead put in her own money, making receipts in the name of all her family members).
Babaji: *Arre,* what is this? I had asked you to collect money from people, to beg for money for the *bhandara.* You seem to have filled all the coupons yourself. Ah! you were embarrassed to ask from others. O, what a pity, you listened to your ego and not to me.
What could have happened if you had asked people? At the most, they would have refused. If they do not wish to give, accept that with equanimity, without hurt feelings. If they give generously, do not feel bloated with pride.
You know, in the beginning, when I started organizing the *bhandara* for *Shivratri,* I too would request a few rich people, to fund the entire event. Then, *Gurumaharaj* appeared in *dhyana* and admonished me, saying, 'What are you up to? A *sadhu* does not get sponsorships; he begs. In addition, make sure that you do not accept more than Rs.100/- from each person.' Since then, I have been collecting money from the smallest of the small and the richest of the rich. I collect money from *panwallas,* rickshaw drivers, bus conductors, police officers and even from poor beggars. Collecting *bhiksha* is a form of

sadhana, to humble the ego. It blesses the receiver and the giver. (Later, Babaji requested *Gurumaharaj,* to lift the ceiling of Rs.100/- and requesting to be allowed, to raise individual contributions especially since he had to start the *gurukul.*)

286. YOU MUST ALWAYS GIVE AN EXTRA RUPEE

Babaji: Come on, out with your wallet. Give me my *bhiksha* for *Shivratri*! (Disciple gives a thousand rupees.)

Babaji: And what about that one rupee? You must always give an extra rupee, when offering money as *bhiksha.*

D: Why?

Babaji: That extra rupee, is a symbol of your ego. Unless you surrender that, what is the use of giving any *dana* or doing any charity?

287. PERFORMING MIRACLES

D: Babaji, tell us some stories of miracles and *chamatkaras.*

Babaji - Why?

D: Those stories are so interesting, as if belonging to another world.

Babaji: Once, after having completed my *sadhana,* I was returning, when, at a place near *Gadhval,* I saw a blind girl. Moved by her plight, I touched her eyes and she regained sight! I fled for dear life. Had I stayed on in that place, they would have turned me into a 'miracle- man', and I would had to spend the rest of my life performing miracles.

288. BABAJI-THE COMPASSIONATE ONE

Often, Babaji would take upon himself, the illnesses of disciples suffering them till they healed. Once, he had taken upon himself, a skin infection, of an old man. The eczema was violent, but Babaji refused to go to a doctor, saying that it would heal in due course. On days when it would flare up, he would say it was because the old man was not following

the diet prescribed to him. Laughingly he would say, '*budha gadbad kar raha hai* – the old man is making mischief.'
All is well that ends well. Mercifully, both Babaji and the old man were completely cured. But what was remarkable, was Babaji's quiet forbearance and compassion.

289. A KIND OF SIDDHI

Babaji's humility was truly touching. He had little attachment to his image or stature, in front of disciples. Once, he said –
Babaji: You know, today I found out, how one can pass through a wall. It's a kind of *siddhi.*
D (excited)**:** Then what happened? Did you try it out? Can you show us how it happens?
Babaji: Well, I asked *Gurumaharaj,* and he sternly admonished, 'Why, are there no doors to the room?'

290. BABAJI EXPLAINS A MIRACLE IN MUMBAI

Some years back, there was a miraculous happening in Mumbai city, when all *Ganapati* images, in temples and homes, started drinking milk, proffered during prayers. The event created a great sensation, scepticism and dialogue among the intellectuals, believers and others. We asked Babaji what the explanation was, to that happening and whether such a thing was possible?
Babaji: Of course it is possible. Human beings cannot accept anything, that does not fit into, their set parameters of thinking, or does not conform to their past experience. But Nature's canvas is vast, with many possibilities. This particular happening is a phenomenon of Nature. It happens once in many centuries, when the planets and *nakshatras* (constellations), are in a particular combination. As soon as these planetary positions will change, this phenomenon will cease.
We did not quite understand the reasoning but saw for a fact that the *Ganapati* images in our homes, actually drank the milk offered to them.

291. GURU KRIPA - THE GRACE OF THE GURU

Babaji generally wrote in English and Hindi. One day, he suddenly started writing verses in *Sanskrit*. Explaining the strange phenomenon to us, he said –

Babaji: With the grace of the *guru,* anything is possible. You know our *shastras* say – 'With the grace of God, even the mute can start speaking and the lame can cross mountains!'

292. DO NOT TAMPER WITH NATURE

Babaji only rarely revealed his yogic powers. On one such occasion when a disciple's mother was seriously ill, Babaji came visiting, but left abruptly. The family was upset at Babaji's abruptness. The old lady was sinking and the end was near. She was restless. The disciple remembered Babaji having mentioned that, anytime he was needed, a disciple could recite the *Lalitasahasranam* and he would come. The disciple sat and recited the *patha.* The next day, Babaji came visiting again.

Having known the old lady from his youthful days, as the wife of his most beloved friend, he felt her pain. He left the *rudrakshamala,* given to him by *Gurumaharaj,* under her pillow and once again, left immediately. The *rudrakshamala* brought relief; soon the old lady passed away. Nevertheless, the disciple was still hurt at Babaji's abruptness and non-participation, when he had visited the hospital.

Babaji (later explained)**:** Her time had come. I wanted her suffering to end. In my presence, the *yamadootas,* would not have been able to do their work. Therefore, I left. It is not right to interfere with the workings of Nature.

293. SOME FAKE HIMALAYAN SADHUS

Babaji loved *malai* or cream. He would always be looking for opportunities to eat it. He would ask for it, with a child-like innocence, unafraid, that it would tarnish his image as a renunciate.

Babaji would often tell a joke, illustrating how *sadhus,* trapped in their image, were always forced to use spiritual truths, to get the pleasures of life –

Babaji: A *sadhu* had gone to collect *bhiksha* (alms). A young lady offered to give him some milk, but of course, she wanted to save the cream for her children. The *sadhu,* tempted at the sight of the cream said, with an air of grave renunciation, 'Let the cream come, don't take the trouble to hold back the *malai.* Let whatever has to come, come. After all, a *sadhu* has no preference.'

At other times, if one offered Babaji *ghee* on his *chapati,* he would laugh and say - '*Arre,* we Himalyan *sadhus* always have our *ghee,* concealed in the *dal* (lentil soup), lest someone see it. Our dry *chapatis,* are in keeping, with our image of austerity and renunciation.'

294. YOU HAVE STILL NOT REALISED

Once, Babaji was taken to meet a god-man, in a small village of Maharashtra. The god-man was highly respected by the villagers. When Babaji reached his house, he sat on his cot and chatted with him. After sometime, Babaji got up, closed his eyes, and placed his hand on the god-man's head.

After a few seconds, in this deeply meditative state, Babaji opened his eyes and told the god-man, 'You have still to realise God. Please continue with your *sadhana.*'

295. 'WINDOW SHOPPING IN SPIRITUAL MATTERS!'

Once, work had taken Babaji to Mumbai for 10-12 days. In Babaji's absence, a disciple who was staying at the *ashram* got bored and decided to go to another *ashram* in Pune, to spend time with the *guru* there.

When Babaji returned, he freshened himself, had his meals and suddenly said, 'What have you not received from the *gurus,* that you still go window-shopping in spiritual matters!

This is a kind of spiritual promiscuousness.' The disciple was speechless at Babaji's clairvoyance.

296. NATURE'S BOOK

Babaji's *ashram* had no toilets. One had to go out in the jungle to ease oneself. Once, he said –

Babaji: Do not go that way; a panther has just gone in that direction.

D: Babaji, how do you know that?

Babaji: That is what this stone is telling me.

D: Babaji, how can a stone tell you something?

Babaji: Nature speaks through its vibrations. You have to be able to read those vibrations. You have to be able to read Nature's book.

At another time, he spoke of how at night, a stone cautioned him to not go in a particular direction. In the morning, wanting to verify the truth in that advice, he went ahead along the path, only to find that, it lead to an abrupt slope, descending into a deep valley.

Babaji had a similar understanding of plants. He would say that, his mother had taught him to talk to plants, so as to understand from them, their usages and properties. You can even hear plants conversing with each other, if you develop the sensitivity to do so. Thus, watering the plants, is also a great service.

297. LIVE AND LET LIVE

At Babaji's old *ashram* at Ambavane, sometimes we slept in the open, in the verandah. Once, on seeing an anthill, a disciple asked Babaji –

D: Babaji, who lives in that?

Babaji: Why do you want to know?

D (laughing)**:** Ah, when you say that, I really want to know. Who is it Babaji?

Babaji: A king Cobra – 14ft. long! It comes at night, hunting for rats, on the roof of my hut. O, many such creatures comprise my family. This poor thing is evident, because of it's size. But it comes, because it enjoys eating rats. It does not come to harm us, so do not worry.

298. BAHADUR BANO – BE FEARLESS

Disciples have walked with Babaji on dark nights, amidst rain and storm, in the jungles of the Himalayas. With him, they have explored the Himalayas unarmed, in the midst of growling tigers, who, to make matters worse, were heard, but not seen. At this point in time, it seems unreal that, in the face of such impending dangers, we could make jokes like, 'Ah! how happy the tiger must be, at the thought of making a sumptuous meal, of Babaji's disciples!'

Babaji's *ashram,* then at Ambavane (near Lonavla), was as if designed to be an exercise in conquering one's fears. In the darkness of the night, he would tell us stories of snakes and tigers that visited the *ashram*. Disciples enjoyed listening to these stories, although visitors were terrified by them. Evidently, his fearlessness rubbed off on us.

At the same time, he cautioned against false bravado and ignoring of simple facts. For example, he would insist that, we should not walk around the *ashram* at night, without a torch and without protecting our feet, lest we stamp on a scorpion or snake. 'Who is at fault if they bite you?' he would ask.

Once, in the dead of the night, hearing some strange sounds, he went deep into the forest, to check things out.

D (to Babaji when he returned)**:** Babaji, were you not afraid?

Babaji: If I had sensed danger, I would not have gone further. One must always be careful, if one senses any physical danger.

D: Babaji, why are we afraid?

Babaji: All fear is only a fear of death. Memory of death, keeps you attached to life. At death, the *pranashakti* (life breath) is as if, squeezed out of the body, as juice is squeezed out of sugarcane. It is a moment of great pain when one's entire life, flashes past in that one moment.Because of this memory, you fear death. Only those who have known Truth and have the grace of the *guru,* can face death.

However, it is moral fearlessness, that needs to be cultivated. Actually, what is feared is the death of the ego, of the petty personality in which we have invested so much, and with which we identify so completely. We are afraid to face the void that will be created, if we let go of our petty likes and dislikes, concepts, ideologies and comforting relationships. To let go of this ego, requires great moral courage. What self-realisation means, is to let this ego die while living. Then you will be reborn in Truth, in this very birth. This courage can only be acquired through *sadhana.* So, take your *sadhana* seriously and cultivate moral fearlessness. Do not be afraid to let your ego die.

There will come a stage in your *sadhana,* when the false personality will loosen. That is a very crucial stage. At that point, *sadhakas* are likely to have no desire to live, because all that they stood for, is burnt to naught. Hold on to the feet of the *guru* and all will be well. Babaji's children are always fearless - *bahadur bano!*

299. BABAJI, AN AUSPICIOUS PRESENCE

Babaji's very presence would alter the inner and outer mood or atmosphere. In fact, disciples in Mumbai, would mark that, as soon as he returned to Mumbai from Lonavla, they would experience a wave of joy, sensing that Babaji had returned.

Once, a family member who had come to meet Babaji, had to leave for Mumbai, late at night. Given that the *ashram* road, was not only rough jungle terrain, but also devoid of any lighting; commuting late at night, was a daunting task, by any standards. Everyone wondered, how the visitor would complete the journey. However, the next time he visited the *ashram,* he narrated how, a mysterious and luminous patch of light guided him all the way to safety and a well-lighted road. Disciples have experienced that in the company of Babaji, their dependence on beverages would vanish. Many have experienced a soothing fragrance linger after he had visited. A deep sense of well-being would descend, upon others, after his visits.

Often times, although he would be physically absent, disciples would smell the distinctive fragrance of his trade-mark Chandrika soap and the coconut oil, with which he used to massage his body, immediately after a bath. Later, when they would meet him, they would inquire – Babaji, did you visit us that day? Babaji would simply smile. If pushed for an answer, he would enigmatically reply – 'I am always with you.'

300. BABAJI'S APARIGRAHA (NON ACQUISITIVENESS)

In his personal life, Babaji lived the principle of non-acquisitiveness. In the initial years, when he rarely met people, he would simply wear a loin cloth. As the human traffic increased, he started wearing a short *dhoti.* Finally when ladies started visiting the *ashram,* he changed his attire to a *lungi* and shawl. At any given time, he only had 2-3 pairs of clothes, consisting of a simple orange *lungi* and an orange shawl.

Once, *Babaji* had to go to Delhi. A disciple purchased a second-class Air Conditioned ticket for him.

D: Babaji, I have purchased a second class Air Conditioned ticket for you this time. You might as well travel in comfort.

Babaji: *Kyun, mere baap ki shadi hai kya!* What's the good occasion - is it my father's marriage or what? Eventually, Babaji returned the ticket to purchase a second-class, ordinary ticket.

Often, while the new *ashram* was under construction, if, when he happened to visit Mumbai, tasty dishes were prepared for him, he would say, 'my children (village workers) are doing back-breaking work there, and here I am enjoying lavish meals.'

No matter how tiring or grueling a day, he would insist on traveling by simple modes of public transport, rarely using a taxi. When purchasing land for the *ashram,* he would walk 20 to 30 kms. daily, in search of a suitable plot of land, as there were no S.T. buses available that would match his schedules. After much persuasion, he acquired a second-hand jeep for the *ashram* work. This too, was used very sparingly, and never for his personal comfort.

Babaji's breakfast consisted of left overs from the previous night, that he shared with the inmates of the *ashram*. Even when he visited our homes, he would insist on first finishing the left overs, before fresh food was made.

Once, disciples at the *ashram,* finished all the breakfast, forgetting to leave some, for the man who helped with the *ashram* work. Babaji curtly chided the disciples and ordered that fresh breakfast be made for the domestic help.

After Babaji left his mortal body, we realised that an office bag for *ashram* papers, a camera, a wristwatch, a wallet, a pair of simple *chappals,* a few pairs of clothes, a bamboo walking stick and the *rudraksha malas* that he wore, were all the property that he possessed. He had no personal money whatsoever. One wonders, if it is possible to have such great moral strength as he did, without the *aparigraha* (non-acquisitiveness) that he practiced.

301. BABAJI AT ELEVATED LEVELS OF CONSCIOUSNESS

Often, Babaji would be at very elevated levels of Consciousness. Sometimes, when we would go to the *ashram,* he would say, 'You know yesterday *Bhagavati* visited me. She stood very shyly outside the door, then came in to chat with me.'

Often times he would say, '*Datta Maharaj* is sitting inside my cottage. Go and spend some time with Him.' At other times his palms would become red and he would say, 'Ah! *Datta Maharaj* has entered me now.' At such times, the divine glow of peace and beauty in his eyes and on his countenance, the spiritually charged atmosphere and the power of those 'happenings', gave us a hint of dimensions of Consciousness that were unknown to us. Those glimpses, however partially comprehended, strengthened our faith inspiring us to intensify our own *sadhana*.

302. I FEEL AS IF I AM SWIMMING IN BLISS

D: Babaji, today you are in such a great mood. I have never seen you so ecstatic.

Babaji (offering the devotee a piece of *jowar* bread and home made butter)**:** I feel as if I am swimming in bliss. Even the treasures of *Indra,* cannot compare, to a moment of inner bliss.

303. WHO CAN UNDERTAKE WORKS?

D: Babaji, why do you want to start an organized *ashram,* wanting me to help run it? You have no worldly desires and I too, have given up my profession, to be with you.

Babaji: Precisely for that reason. Only those that have no desire to cash in on their work, no vested motive, must undertake such works.

304. NOBODY WANTS GOD

Babaji (On returning home, after a fund raising spree)**:** Nobody really wants God; everybody only wants money.

305. THE SATTVA IN MONEY

Once, while raising funds for the *ashram* project, Babaji was visiting *Velapur.* He stayed with disciples, while people from the neighbouring homes came to meet him. Some offered *bhiksha* of Rs.100/-, some more, and others a little less. Suddenly, a poor old woman came and gave him a rupee coin, as her contribution. Touched to the core, Babaji held the rupee coin in one hand, and a hundred rupee note in the other, saying –

Babaji: Don't underestimate the power of this single rupee, it is equal in potency to the hundred rupees. It is the *sattva* in the money, that gives it value. It is how you earn the money, and the sentiment behind the act of charity, that gives value to the money.

306. GURUS ARE NOT SERVANTS

D: Babaji, since the *gurus* have asked you to create this *ashram*, why don't you ask them to also send you the funds, instead of getting stressed and running here and there for the same?
Babaji: They are *gurus*. They are not my servants. They will do what needs to be done.

307. GURU - AS AN ORDINARY MAN

Babaji: You know, I am the representative of the *gurumandala*. Anything that I say, taking the name of *Gurumaharaj*, has to happen, as then, the entire power of the *gurumandala*, starts operating.
D: In that case Babaji, why are you running here and there, for this *Shaktiyogashrama gurukul* project; just call upon *Gurumaharaj* to get it done.
Babaji: I have taken up this *ashram* work, in my individual capacity, to address a social need. Although they support every thing that I undertake; this work has been undertaken by me, as an ordinary man.
D: Then, what is the work of the *gurus*?
Babaji: To uplift souls, that is all.

308. OBSTACLES ARE A PART OF WORK

While working on the gurukul project, many times *Babaji* was badly injured. So once, during meditation, he asked *Gurumaharaj*, 'Why am I meeting with so many accidents nowadays, this never used to happen before?'
Gurumaharaj said, 'You never undertook any work before. If

one undertakes works, obstacles are bound to arise.'

309. BABAJI'S COMPASSION

When Babaji started the *ashram* work, all energies were spent on raising funds, meeting people and making plans and projects. He had little time to guide disciples. Once, a disciple asked -

D: Babaji, your journey is over. But what about me, I don't find any time for *sadhana* and you have no time to guide?

Babaji: *Arre* don't worry. I will do *sadhana* for you. What are my *sadhanas* for? They are for you people. What use do I have of them now?

D: Babaji, you found the Truth after so many hardships and rigorous *sadhanas,* and here we are, chatting, joking and eating merrily with you; while you share the Truth with us.

Babaji: It is all the fruits of one's *karma.*

Actually, it was only out of compassion, that he gave us so much, without any effort on our part. It is only now, that disciples realise his great magnanimity and compassion.

310. MASTERS NEVER DIE

Many years back, when he had divined the date of his passing away, he came over to take final leave. The disciple looked at him with tears in her eyes.

Babaji: I seem to have wasted my teachings on you. You still see me just as this body. Ah! You have missed the point. Masters never die, they live forever through their teachings, in the hearts of disciples.

(Fortunately for us, he was able to gain a few more years then, by the grace of *Gurumaharaj*.)

311."MAKE MY SAMADHI THERE."

After Babaji shed his mortal body, the disciples were wondering where, Babaji's *samadhi* should be erected.

One of the village women from the village revealed - 'You know one day, when we were working on site, Babaji suddenly said, 'See this *audumbara tree*; when I pass away, make my *samadhi* there.'
Today, Babaji's *samadhi,* stands at that very place.

~

And finally, his parting message at all times, to one and all -

'khush raho! shivoum – Be happy, *shivoum.'*

D: Babaji, what is the meaning of *shivoum*?

Babaji: All is *shiva* – auspicious, sacred, unblemished and free (Babaji prepares to take leave.)

D: Just a moment Babaji, let me bow down to you.

Babaji: Bow down to your very Self. I am That.

~

॥ शिवोऽम् ॥

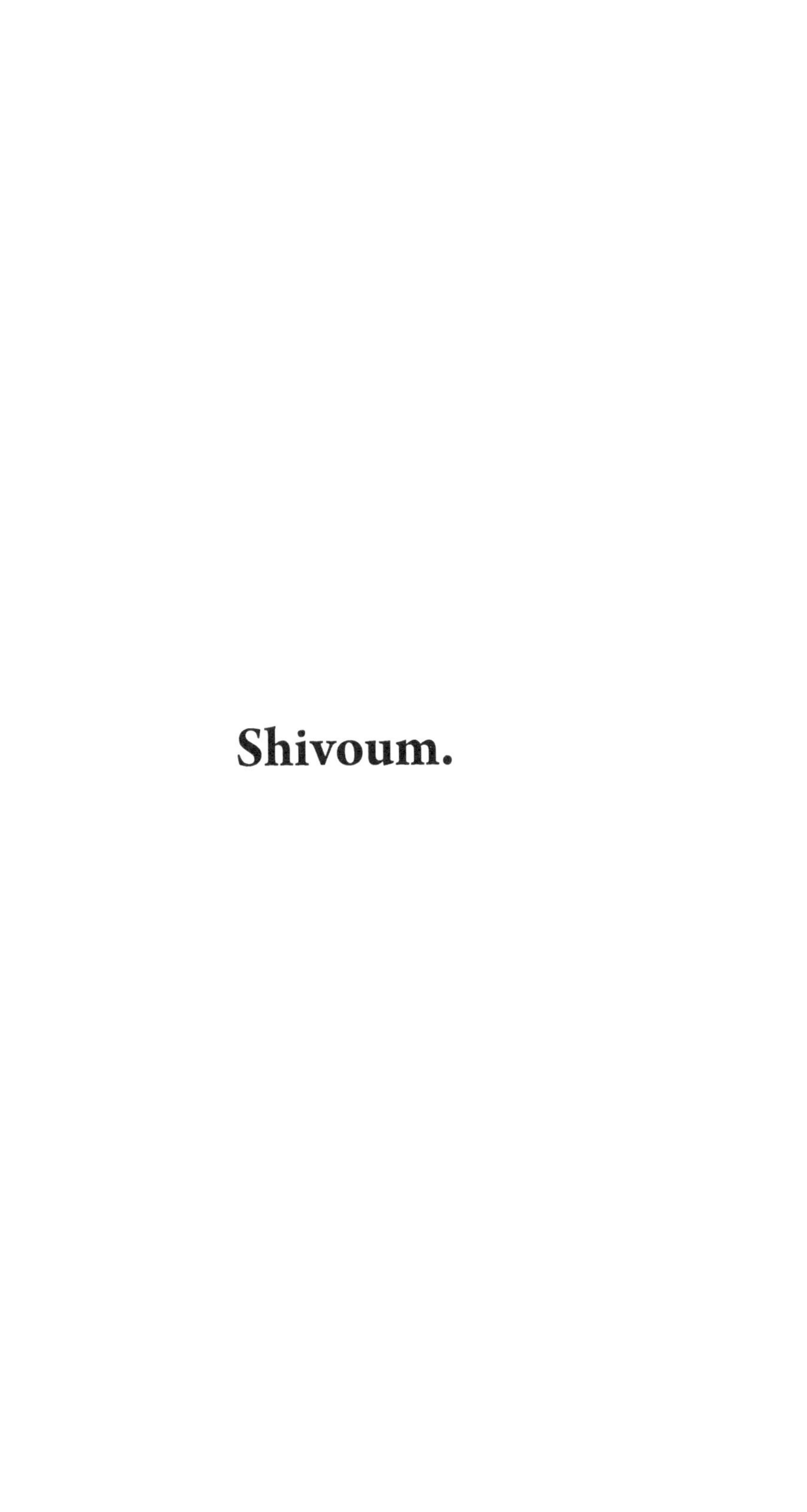

Shivoum.

A Vision Of Education

An ashramite lives in the company of the 'Self',
An ashramite recognises that there is
none other than the 'Self'.
An ashramite lives and works in
discipline & moderation.
An ashramite is friendly with his own mind and body.
An ashramite complains not about another's.
So, is the ashramite a joyless bloke?
You will find out when you become an ashramite!

~

A VISION OF EDUCATION

Babaji spent the last couple of years of his life striving to set up the ashram-gurukul, at village of Telbaila. Although, the idea had been simmering in his mind ever since he came back from the Himalayas, it was only in the last few years of his life that he worked towards it.

One day, Babaji walked in with a roll of papers under his arm. 'Sign here', he commanded. Meekly, the disciple signed the papers before she dared to ask –

D: What are these papers Babaji?

Babaji: O, these are the trust deed papers of our ashram-gurukul.

D: You mean ... ?

Babaji: Yes, we are going ahead with the plans. I have had all the legal documents prepared. (Laughing) In fact the officer on duty was most encouraging and said, 'Babaji, go ahead. In this country, only crooked politicians and selfless fakirs can get anything done!'

D: But Babaji, you are a simple fakir with few wants and with no ambitions or desires. So, why are you undertaking these difficult projects?

Babaji: Precisely. Those who have no vested interests alone can undertake God's work. This ashram-gurukul is God's work, it is the need of the hour; it is not for any personal gain, material or psychological.

Arre, does it not pain you to see these children burdened by an education system, that is lopsided and lacking in holism; a system, which is callously indifferent, to the inner growth of an individual, a system which creates cultural orphans, while wholly neglecting the spiritual ingredient in education. This education system is only information gathering and not man-making.

Does it not pain you to see our ancient arts and sciences languishing? Either they are misinterpreted or they are ignored; I don't know which is worse. Look at the classical arts – they were meant to be sadhanas to achieve the highest Truth, to see God. Today, they have become accomplishments and slick professions or worse still, forms of entertainment.

Look at our sciences of ayurveda and jyotisha shastra; they were meant to understand the mysteries and secrets of Nature and designed to help us live in tune with Nature. Don't you feel that we must help to preserve these sciences? And above all, look at this mother of all arts and sciences – yoga. It has understood Nature from deeply meditative states perfecting every system of physical, psychological and psychical discipline, to integrate the human being allowing him to experience expanded states of Consciousness.

Are you going to allow these treasures of the human race to pass away into oblivion? Don't you feel, that these must be taught to children and young minds, as a part of their education? Isn't it a pity, that education is conceived as a means of livelihood only, and not as a means to enrich and emancipate the personality? Education, is not for earning 'bread' alone..

D: But, isn't that how every parent plans his child's life and career? At first schooling, then graduation/post graduation till finally the journey ends, with a good job.

Babaji: One of the faultiest ideals that the current education system puts before us is that, to earn well, is the be-all and end-all of existence. Such a person is all 'clever and conniving brain'; out of touch with body and spirit. Such an ideal will breed human beings who are worldly-wise and egotistical. The greatest loss here being, a loss of sensitivity to one's inner self, to nature and to life. These children will be poor from within, no matter how rich their lives may be from the outside. If we are not careful, this materialism, ambition and over use of the mind, will be the undoing of the human race.

On the other hand, look at the lofty vision of education that our ancient civilisation has. Our rishis would say, 'that is knowledge (education), which emancipates - *vidya sa ya vimuktaya*.' We have to revive that grand vision of education. Even if nobody helps me, I am going to go ahead and do my bit!

D: Arre Babaji, don't get angry; I am only trying to understand this new goal that has so consumed you. So how do you propose to give shape to this vision?

Babaji: See, my dream is to create a mini-university of the four classical arts of sculpture (*shilpa*), painting (*chitra*), architecture (*vastu*) and dance (*nritya*), and the classical science of longevity (*ayurveda*), the science of astrology (*jyotisha*) and the science of mind-body integration and Self-realisation (yoga). It will be called the '*Sapta Bharati*.' At the hub of the Sapta Bharati, will be a school for children, so that children are nurtured in an invigorating climate of spirituality and creativity. There is no point in trying to reform the older generation. It is the new crop that we have to protect and nurture.

D: What will be the vision behind the school?

Babaji: 'Sher ke bacche paida karenge – We will create a bold new generation.' These children will be physically strong, mentally alert, emotionally alive and spiritually inclined. We will create a generation which will be strong and sensitive, with their heads and their hearts integrated. They will work with their hands, while being anchored in the spirit.

D: But Babaji, how will you translate this into a workable syllabus?

Babaji: Education is essentially a process of self-revelation, self-expression and self-exploration, rather than a standard programme where one is 'told' or 'informed.' The rich and dynamic fiber of life, cannot be reduced to dry and boring facts. It's ever changing beauty has to be experienced. Education is a process of liberation; a school provides only an atmosphere conducive to inner freedom and enrichment. All subjects and syllabi are only means to that end.

D: I understand. But how will this vision, be translated into an education programme?

Babaji: Well, training in music/dance and martial arts will be compulsory so that, they will be sensitive, while being strong. Pottery, carpentry, weaving and the crafts, as also engineering skills, will train them to translate concepts, visions and creative ideas into actuality; so that they do not remain intellectual dilettantes who talk big but can do nothing. These simple disciplines are very effective in character building, because they teach you to execute what you intuit or conceive. They help to integrate the mind and body. It is the lack of emphasis on these, that makes modern education hollow and incomplete. The current education system may help a student to get a white- collor job, but his/her personality may still not be integrated.

D: Arre Babaji, these children are already so over burdened; where will they find the time for these fringe activities?

Babaji(sternly): These are not fringe activities. I repeat; they are character building. It is because, firstly, you think that education is only about academics, and secondly because you think of education as a means to 'bread and butter' alone, that you relegate these activities, to a secondary position. As for the problem of overburdening; these children are stressed because their energy levels are very low. A young mind can cope with many challenges, if the reservoir of energies is built up through sadhana. How?

Babaji: At the ashram-gurukul, the day will begin and end with aumkara sadhana. This will raise energies that are dissipated and scattered in the lower centers, to elevate Consciousness.

When these subtle energies are raised, bookish knowledge and all your academic syllabi will be literally, child's play.

D: But Babaji, people feel that values of cultural rootedness and spiritual orientation are old-fashioned, even out of tune with the modern, scientific age.

Babaji: If education is a process of flowering and blooming, then it has to be rooted in a soil, in a culture. The current education system is totally Western oriented. It produces children who are cultural orphans, creating a nation of ungrateful, unfaithful offspring. Children growing with such fake and assumed identities, can only break from within at the least unsettling occurrence. Education is a way of thinking, feeling and living. Even modes of dress, eating, and etiquette, should not be seen as the trivialities of a culture, but rather as the essential expression of its inherent philosophy and world-view. They are the rich raiment of a culture, nestling its soul. Only a student rooted in the rich values of his own culture, can be truly open to other cultures. If we teach a child religious *stotras* or traditional prayers, it is only to awaken them to the purity of their own being, or shall I say, of all beings.

As for spirituality, it can never be the cause of any conflict. See how our Bhagavati is described – '*navanam puranam adhisham sugatrim* – She, the graceful limbed one, is the Empress of the old and the new.' The old and the new are but Her manifestation. These children will be equally well versed in the modern sciences as well as modern modes of living. They will have expertise in computer science, as well as all other modern sciences. Why, if I will make them live the natural, ashram life, I will also give them a taste of opulence and luxury. I am not averse to giving them even an experience of a five-star hotel! *Sher ke bacche kisi chij se darte nahin* – freedom is to fear nothing, to have the strength to remain untouched and pure under all circumstances. This fearless attitude can be cultivated in childhood.

D: What about academics Babaji? Man does not live by bread alone yet, that is important.
Babaji: Why, of course, we will get ourselves affiliated to a recognized Board of Education so that, these children have academic qualifications and certifications to get by in the world, to join the main stream. When you have learnt to climb a mountain, walking on a flat surface is easy. In essence, I believe that children should learn to live free off the orthodox and the unorthodox, the modern and the traditional, the conventional and the unconventional values, for in themselves, none of these are of any consequence. A rigid adherence to any of these values can only result in dogmatism and stagnation, while life is a flowing river. All concepts and ideals – traditional or modern – are only tools and instruments, to attain the supreme good in life. It is in this spirit, that the traditional vidyas will be imparted to the student. We do not want to bring back the old times, but to usher in a new time, the eternal values.
D: Phew Babaji! This is a daunting vision.
Babaji: So get ready to start the work.
D: How?
Babaji: First of all, draft a brochure that will elucidate the key concepts of this vision of education, while I go and collect some *bhiksha* (alms) for the ashram.
D: Babaji, then what happens to my spiritual sadhana?
Babaji: This is also sadhana.
This was Babaji in a new incarnation, an incarnation that in turn baffled, confused, impressed, awed and even met with the disapproval of disciples. It was so strikingly different from the image he hitherto had of a playful fakir, that at times, it was hard to recognise him as the same person. It also revealed the dynamism and flexibility of a personality, that refused to be slotted in any category, a personality that was completely unafraid to break images, even of himself.
Gone was the cloth 'jhola' that he carried to keep his knick-

knacks. In its place was a plastic folder, to be substituted later, by a brief case (gifted by disciples) with important papers, appeals for donations, brochures, list of people to be contacted...simple marketing tools, made effective by a childlike and passionate faith in his project.

All conversations henceforth were dominated by the ashram gurukul project. Visits to Mumbai were spent in brain storming on the project with educationists, disciples and any one who was inspired by the project, in collecting funds, in visualising the architectural designs of the gurukul and in deep introspection, on the other details of the ashram- gurukul. Back at the ashram, all time was spent in hunting for a suitable location for the new ashram-gurukul complex. He would walk 20-30 kms daily, scouting for land, getting estimates of land prices and weighing the pros and cons of different locations. He finally acquired a sizeable plot of land in Telbaila village, Maharashtra.

Very soon, he started building the first ashram structures, in the remote jungle. Once a visitor, on coming to the new ashram –

Visitor: Babaji, to what god-forsaken place have you brought me?

Babaji (laughing uncontrollably): How can Bhagvati's ashram be God forsaken!

Visitor: Babaji, you need support to undertake this project.

Babaji: Here Bhagavati is the only support; She will do what is necessary.

His methods of fund raising were simple - a guileless persistence and unabashed begging. Like a child begging for a toy from his parents, he would by turns, persuasively appeal or obstinately demand donations. Every day, on returning home, he would share the triumphs of the day gleefully, so much so that a disciple would jokingly ask him –

D: So Babaji, what are the loot figures for today?

Babaji (giggling): Arre you call them loot figures, these are *bhiksha!*

Not all experiences would be so pleasant –

There would be rejections of appeals for donations, breach of promises and even indifference to the project. This brush with worldly-minded people and their attachment to their wealth, often made him comment, 'Every body wants money, nobody wants God or peace of mind!' There would be practical problems on site like for example, labour trouble, or water shortage. The only source of water was a privately owned but abandoned spring nearby. Babaji had no choice but to use the water from that spring.

A visitor once asked –
Visitor: Babaji, does this not amount to stealing, since the spring is not on your land?
Babaji: Water belongs to God. Besides at the moment nobody is using that plot of land or water, so I am not depriving or usurping anybody's share.
Out of touch with paper work, official business and networking skills, he would often exhaust himself in doing small tasks. Modestly he would confess – I have forgotten business practices but I shall regain them.
There was a major illness; there were threats to life in the form of, snakebites, scorpion bites, road accidents, and other minor and major injuries. With touching humanness, he once asked *Gurumaharaj* –
Babaji: Why are so many obstructions coming in my way now, this never used to happen before?
Gurumaharaj: Well, you never undertook such work before, so how can there be obstructions? Set backs are a part of work.
Gurumaharaj's insightful and gentle chiding was enough to

renew his zeal.
In the past, when disciples would suggest that he have a gobar gas plant at the *ashram* or start cultivating roses, he would laugh and say – 'What, have I become a Babaji to start a gobar gas plant? You know the story of how, the acquisition of one loin cloth triggered a chain of events, that made a *sadhu* into a *grihasthi* ? Do you want me to go the same way?'

But now, as if to bring home the fact that, the end justifies the means, he was open to every scheme of rural development and fund-raising, every new idea on educational modules. The final endorsement of Babaji's new *avatara* or incarnation came when, one day, after a meditation camp at the new *ashram* –
Babaji: Let's make a structured time-table for the camps.
This, coming from Babaji, who hitherto only acted spontaneously, being averse to structure & habit; took the disciple by surprise.
D (With an amused expression): And who will follow it, will you be able to adhere to it?
Babaji (with humility): Yes, yes, I promise I will. This endeavor will require structure and discipline.

For a bohemian fakir like Babaji, this simple commitment was the greatest expression of his surrender to the project.
A couple of days before he passed away he said, 'I have done what I could, now you do what you feel needs to be done.'

Thus ended an era at Shaktiyogashrama.

Glossary

abhyasa - intense study
adhyatma - a study of the Self or spiritual studies
adnyana - ignorance
advaita - one of the six schools of philosophy, which believes that, only Conciousness is real, the rest is illusion
advaita bhava - an unbroken feeling that, all is One
aghori baba - a practitioner of the aghora sect
ahamkara - the ego
ajapajapa- the continuous, unheard and automatic chanting of the 'hamsa' mantra, that happens in all human beings
ajna chakra - the centre in the space between the eye-brows
akasha tattva - of the five elements, the element of ether
Allah - Supreme Godhead in Islam
amavashya - the night of new moon
apsara - water nymphs
asana - physical postures in yoga sadhana
ashram - communes created by spiritual masters, to provide an environment for self-growth
archana - refer 'puja'
Audumbara tree - a tree that is associated with the deity Dattatreya
aum, aumkara - sacred syllable, akin to 'amen'
Avadhoota Gita - a sacred text ascribed to Shri Avadhoota Dattatreya, also refered to as Datta Gita, it is the highest expression of Hindu mystical and non-dualistic thought
avataras - incarnations
Ayodhya - geographically, a place by the same name in North India. In the Ramayana, the kingdom of Rama and symbolically, the body
ayurveda - the ancient Indian science of longevity and healing

bahadur - brave
beta - son
Bhagavati - a name of the Goddess

Bhagvad Gita - a sacred text of the Hindus, that is in the form of a dialogue between the warrior Arjuna and Lord Krishna. It advocates the value of dispassionate work
Bhagvat purana - One of the eighteen major puranas or sacred legends
bhajan - hymn
bhakta- devotee
bhakti yoga - the science and practice of uniting with God through devotion
bhandara - distribution of food for free, as a part of religious ceremonies
Bhandasura - demon of lethargy/sloth/sluggishness
bhava - devotion/mood
bhiksha - alms
bhogi - one who enjoys sense pleasures
bhoot - ghost
Brahma - In the trininty of Gods; the Creator in the trininty of Gods
brahmacharya - commonly understood as celebacy;
hidden meaning - to reside in Truth
brahman - Absolute, indivisible Consciousness
brahmarandhra - the highest center of Consciousness at the top of the head
buddhi - Intellect

chaitanya - Consciousness
chakra - centre of Consciousness
chamatkar - miracle
chapatti - unleavened, whole wheat bread
chintana - deep thinking
chitta - the platform of Consciousness
chulha - Indian stove
cosmic mind - the sum total of all human ideas and insights

dal - lentil
dana - charity
dargah - tombs of Muslim saints
dasi - servant

Dattatreya / DattaMaharaj - godhead who is a coming together of the trinity of the Hindu pantheon - Brahma, Vishnu, Shiva. He is the author of the Avadhoota Gita
deva - God
devi - the Goddess
dhairya - fortitude
dharma - lit. duty, flow of one's being
dhobighat - a place where clothes are put for drying
dhoti - draped apparel for men
dhyana - an undivided state of Consciousness where the distinction between knower and known drops
diksha - initiation
dnyana - Knowledge
duhkha bhava - any feeling of sorrow
dvaita / dwaita - duality

ekadashi - a day of fasting, on the eleventh day of a lunar cycle
ekagrata - single pointedness of the mind
ekanta sadhana - spiritual practices that are done in absolute solitude, under the guidance of a spiritual master
ekatma - oneness
ekrasa - oneness

fakir - bohemian saint

Gajamukha / Gajanana - the elephant headed God, Ganapati
Ganapati - the Hindu God who destroys obstacles
ghee - clarified butter
Girija - a name of Parvati, lit. daughter of the mountain
Gorakshanatha - great yogi, looked upon as a super human teacher and even as a deity, known for the performance of fantastic yogic miracles
granthas - religious scriptures
granthis - physic knots
grihasthi - household
GudiPadwa - festival in April also considered by some to be the new year

gurave namah - I bow down to the guru
guru- a spiritual master who removes the darkness of ignorance with the light of ultimate knowledge
gurucharitra - the life and teachings of a guru
gurukul - the place where a guru lives with his family of disciples, to study spiritual practices or other forms of knowledge
guruma - the guru's wife
Gurumaharaja - literally, the great guru, it was how Babaji addressed his master
gurumandala - the lineage of gurus
gurumukha - the countenance of the guru
guruseva - service to the guru
guru tattva - the essence of the guru i.e. the Self
hamsa mantra -the syllables 'ham' and 'sah', that are ceaselessly chanted by the incoming and outgoing breath
Indra - king of the Gods
ishmaya - immersed in God
ishta devta - personal God
Ishvar - the highest, one God

Japa - recitation of mantra
Jiva - individual / embodied Consciousness
Jnaneshvari - a sacred text, which is a commentary on the Bhagavad Gita, written by a 12th century Indian saint, called Jnaneshvara
Kabir - a medieval, mystical saint, from North India in the mediaeval times
Kalpa-vriksha- wish fulfulling tree
Kamashakti - primordial energy
karma - deeds
karmic account - the record of one's deeds
khichadi - rice and lentil preparation
kirtan - songs in praise of the glory of God
Krishna - a popular Hindu god, considered to be a total embodiment of Supreme Consciousness
kshatriya - of the four classes - the warrior class
kumkum - vermillion

kundalini shakti - primordial energy in an individual, that lies coiled at the base of the spine
kurta - Indian shirt, for men

laddu - ball of sweet / sweetheart
Lalitasahsranama - a sacred text containing the thousand names of the Goddess
Lanka - geographically present day Sri Lanka, in mythology the kingdom of the demon king Ravana
lokas - the different planes of existence like heaven, earth and underworld
lungi - sarong

madira - lit. alchoholic drinks; also a term for spiritual practices involving intoxicants
mahasamadhi - the final merging with Supreme Consciousness, on shedding the body
Maha Vishnu - One of the Gods of the trinity; He plays the role of The Sustainer
Mahishasura - a demon in the form of a buffalo, having the powers to change his form at will
maithuna - sexual union, here as a part of tantric practices
'm'akara - five ritualistic practices in the tantras, beginning with the alphabet 'ma'
malai - whole cream
mamsa - spiritual practices involving eating of meat
manana - cogitation
mangala sutra - auspicious thread/chain worn as sign of marriage
Manipur chakra - centre of Conciousness at the navel
mantra - sound vibration or syllable that has energising and purifying properties
mantra diksha - initiating an aspirant by giving a mantra
mantra sadhana - spiritual practice that requires the chanting of mantras or sound notes and syllables
matsya - spiritual practices involving eating of fish
maya - the world of illusion and dualistic opposing tendencies
mirabai - a medeival saint poetess, from a royal family of Rajasthan

mohini vidya - a form of black magic that can ensnare, enslave, kill or cause harm to those on whom it is practiced
moong dal - yellow lentil
mudra - ritualistic hand gestures
mukti - liberation
muladhara chakra - the center of Consciousness at the root of the genitals
mula svabhava - eternal nature

Narada - great sage and devotee of Maha Vishnu, known to be mischievous
natha - a sect of yogis, i.e natha yogis who were worshippers of Shiva
navaratri - festival of nine days in October, in honour of the Goddess
nirupaya diksha - a form of spiritual initiation

padmasana - the lotus position for sitting in meditation
pakodas - a fried Indian snack in the form of dumplings
pancha mahabhutas - the five elements of earth, water, fire, air and ether
panch makaras - the five forms of worship in the tantras
panwallas - those who sell betel leaves, an Indian mouth freshner
Paramartha - the highest meaning or purpose of life i.e. to merge with God
Paramatma - The highest Soul or Supreme Consciousness
parayana - reading of sacred texts from beginning to end in a specified time frame
Parvati - the consort of Shiva
patha - the chanting of devotional verses
pradakshina - circumambulation
pramada - lethargy
pranas - the life breath that pervades the body in five forms
pranava sadhana - the spiritual practice of reciting the sacred syllable 'aum'
pranshakti - life energy
prapancha - illusory world / universe
prasada - lit. food offering made to God, symbolically grace

puja - the ritual of communication with God through lighting of lamps and incense and other such ways of welcoming and tuning in to the diety

Rabia - a sufi saint (female) from the 12th century, from Turkestan
rajayoga - the science of union with God through discrimination and devotion
Rama - refer Ramayana
ramrajya - the kingdom of Rama, symbolically the kingdom of peace
Ramayana - one of the two important epics of Hindu mythology. It is the story of the protagonist Rama, his brother Lakshmana and consort Sita and his combat with the demon Ravana.
Ravana - refer Ramayana
Ravana dahana - burning of Ravana
Ravidas - a mystical saint poet who was the guru of Mirabai
rudraksha mala - a necklace made of rudraksha beads

sadashiva - lit. a name of shiva, symbolically an unbroken state of Conciousness without modifications
sadhaka - spiritual aspirant
sadhana - spiritual practices
sadhu - monk
sahasranama - the thousand names of Gods
Sahasrar Padma / chakra - centre of Conciousness at the top of the head
sakshat - first hand and tangible experience
samarpana - surrender
samkhya - one of the six syatems of Indian philosophy founded by Kapila, that understands the world as being born of the union of Purusha and Prakriti
sampradaya - oral traditions
samsara - the changing world of names and forms
samsari - worldly minded
samyak samadhi - highest non-dualistic experience of Consciousness
sandhikalas - the times of the day that serve as links in the cosmic time i.e sunrise and sunset

sanyasa diksha - the final initiation when the aspirant is initiated into monk-hood
sanyasa - renunciation of the worldly life and devoting onesself wholly to spritual practices
sanyasi - monk
sat-asat viveka buddhi - the discriminative faculty that can distinguish between Truth and Untruth
sat-chit-ananda - Truth-Consciousness-Bliss. A state of complete integration-the final state in self- realisation
satori - awakening, a term from Zen Buddhism
sattva - one of the three qualities of matter closest to undivided Consciousness
shakta diksha - another form of initiation
shaktipat diksha - a form of initiation where the guru transmits his positive energies to the disciple
shaktis - energies
shaktiyoga - same as raja yoga
shambhavi diksha - a form of initiation
Shanakaracharya - founder of the Advaita school of philosophy in the 9th century
shastras - sciences
shisya - disciple
Shiva - the third God of the Hindu Trinity who dissolves the cosmos
shivoum - all is Shiva
shivratri - the 'Night of Awakening' in which Shiva, the Auspicious God, is deeply felt
shloka - Sanskrit verses
shraddha - faith
shringara - the pinnacle of joyous experience especially known to be found in sexual experience
shri vidya - ritual practices involving the worship of the Goddess through the sixteen syllabled mantra and the shri yantra
shri yantra - cosmic diagram
siddha - a realised soul
siddhi - spiritual powers gathered through spiritual practices
sita - refer Ramayana

soham - I am that
strotras - sacred verses
subhashitas - poetic couplets to inculcate values and wisdom
sufi - a practitioner of Sufism, Islamic mysticism
sushumna - vital nerve in the spine through which higher energies have to be passed and raised
svabhava - intrinsic nature
swami - a renunciate

tamasik - gross tendencies towards sloth and inertia
tantra - texts on spiritual sciences, that include ritual & other esoteric practices, to raise Consciousness. They can be Shaivite Tantras or Shakta Tantras
tapas - burning/purifying one's energies, to unite with God
tika - mark on the forehead
tup - refer to ghee
tur dal - lentil

upanishad - sacred texts that are the last part of the Vedas. Literally means 'to sit beside' the Truth or Guru
upaya - means

vairagya - non-attachment
varkari sampradaya - an oral tradition which believes that, union with god can be achieved, through chanting of sacred hyms, penned by the saint poets of Maharashtra
vedas - the sacred and oldest texts of the Hindus
vibhakta - not seperated from god or integrated with god
vidya - esoteric sciences
Vishudhi chakra - centre of Conciousness at the throat
vishvamitra - a great sage
Vitthala - a form of Vishnu, one of the Trinity
viveka - discrimination between Truth and untruth

yantra - potent geometric configurations or diagrams that are used in worship
yamdoot - the messengers of the God of Death

yatra - pilgrimage
yoga - the science of Self-realisation involving physco-physical practices
yoga sadhana - spiritual practices of yoga
yogi - the integrated one
yogini - a woman who is integrated with God

Translations and Texts from...

Avadhoota Gita - with English translation by Shree Purohit Swami
Edited by - Shankar Mokashi - Punekar (M.A. , Ph.D)
Munshi Manoharlal Publishers Pvt. Ltd - 1979

Ashtavakra Samhita - by Swami Nityaswarupananda
Advaita Ashrama, Calcutta - 1987

Sankara The Missionary
Central Chinmaya Mission Trust - 1978

Shri Lalita Sahasranama Stotram
Shri Ramakrishna Math - Mylapore

Shri Lalita Sahasranama
With introduction and commentary by C. Suryanarayana Murthy
Bharatiya Vidya Bhavan, 5th edition - 2000

गुरु चेला सुख सों बसें
निसि दिन प्रभु आधीन।
एक गुरु में व्यस्त है
एक प्रभु में लीन॥

Swami H. Madhukar

गुरु चेला सुख सों बसें
निसि दिन प्रभु आधीन।
एक गुरु में व्यस्त है
एक प्रभु में लीन॥

स्वामी हरिमधुकर

Picture Gallery

SWAMI SHRI HARISH MADHUKAR
"BABAJI"

THE BEGINNINGS

The debonair art critic / media person / business man.

With his beautiful wife Smt.Nalini Lahir.

ENJOYED THE PLEASURES OF LIFE AND YET THERE WAS A SEARCH FOR THE 'BEYOND'.

Participating in pujas...

Reading and discussing for endless hours, in seclusion, with close friend and well known artist, Shri Govind Solegaonkar.

THE JOURNEY WITHIN BEGINS...

AND CULMINATES IN TOTAL FREEDOM AND JOY.

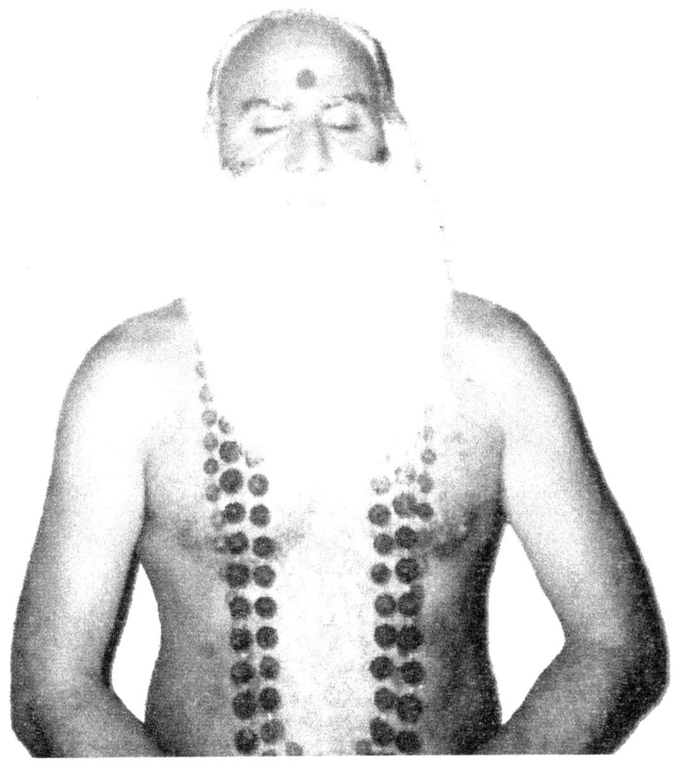

HE ENJOYED EVERYTHING - FROM THE
STILLNESS OF MEDITATION...

...TO THE EXPRESSIONS OF LIFE.

In the stable with his horses.

Feeding the ducks - a daily ritual.

Dancing with villagers on Mahashivaratri.

Sharing with children.

Cooking for his 'children'.

LOVE AND JOY IS ALL THAT HE KNEW

Exploring village
Telbaila for the Gurukul.

An informal meditation camp for children of disciples.

He knew no caste or creed.

IN THE HIMALAYAS

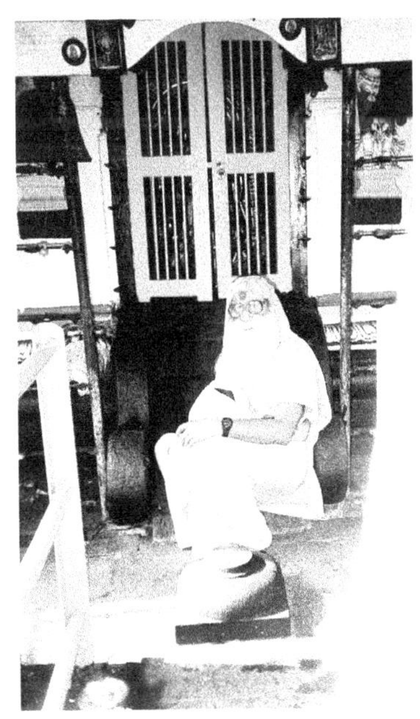

GROOMING DISCIPLES ON THE HIMALAYAN TREK

WITH FAMILY

With wife and grand-daughter.

With wife and close family friends.

With daughter and sister.

With family, at the inauguration of Shaktiyogashrama Gurukulam.

THE MASTER IN VARIOUS MOODS...

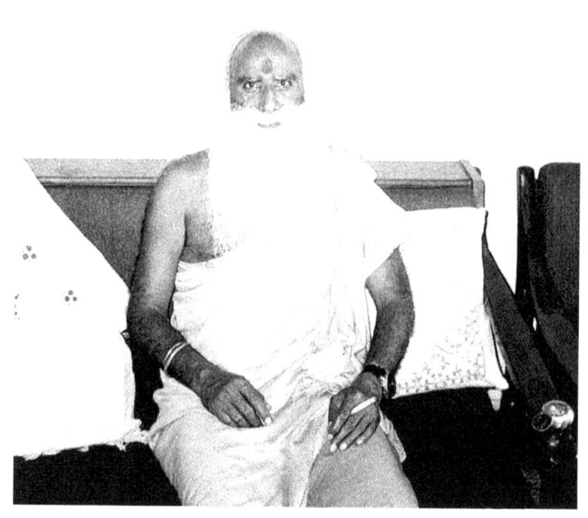

THE SACRED RELICS OF THE MASTER.

The rudraksha mala given by Gurumaharaj.

The sacred Shankha of Gurumaharaj.

The Padukas.

THE INTERIORS OF BABAJI'S KUTIR.

The bed, the stick and the chappals that he used.

THE SAMADHI

"शिवोऽम्"
"शिवोऽम्"

वर्तमान मेरी काया और भविष्य मेरी दृष्टि है। अतीत
मेरी छाया मात्र है।
मैं न सोता हूँ और न जागता हूँ। न खोता हूँ और न
पाता हूँ। मैं होते हुए भी नहीं हूँ और न होते हुए भी इस सम्पूर्ण
विश्व में अखण्ड भाव से व्याप्त हूँ।
जो मुझे जानता है वह अपने आप को नहीं जानता और
जो अपने आप को जानता है वह मेरे साथ एकात्म भाव में
समासीन है।
स्वामी श्री हरीश मधुकर
२७-८-१९२३ — ३१-१०-१९९६

SAMADHI EPITHET

मैं इस साधारण मनुष्य रूप में साक्षात् अकाल पुरूष हूँ जिस
में मेरेपन का कोई भाव नहीं । यह विश्व मेरी सत्ता है और मैं
सभी में अविच्छिन्न रूप से ओतप्रोत हूँ ।

वर्तमान मेरी काया और भविष्य मेरी दृष्टि है ।
अतीत मेरी छाया मात्र है ।

मैं न सोता हूँ और न जागता हूँ। न खोता हूँ और न पाता हूँ ।
मैं होते हुए भी नहीं हूँ और न होते हुए भी इस
सम्पूर्ण विश्व में अखण्ड भाव से व्याप्त हूँ ।

जो मुझे जानता है वह अपने आप को नहीं जानता
और जो अपने आप को जानता है वह मेरे साथ एकात्म भाव में समासीन है ।

॥ शिवो३म् ॥

SAMADHI EPITHET

In this ordinary human form, I am the very
Immortal Being *(purusha)*, in whom there is no
feeling of 'mineness'.
This universe is 'My' domain and 'I' pervade
everything in my purest form.

The 'present'is my body, the 'future' my vision and
the 'past', is only my shadow.

I am neither asleep nor awake, have nothing to gain or lose.
I 'am', yet I 'am not', and yet again, I pervade this entire
universe, in a state of perfection.

He who knows 'me' (this mortal man), does
not know his Self.
And he, who knows his Self, is established in
me, in a state of Oneness.

Shivoum

THE ASHRAM

The presiding deity - Bhagavati.

The visionary - Babaji.

Inaugurating the Shaktiyogashrama Gurukulam.

THE PREMISES

Babaji's Kutir

The Ashram pathway.

The residential cottages.

The open air stage.

THE PROJECTS - Cultural Awareness Camps

Childrens Camps

FESTIVALS

Shaktimahotsava, Annual Spring Festival (February - March)

Sharadotsava, Annual Autumn Festival (October)

Nateshvari Dance Gurukul - Mumbai

(An expression of Swami Shri Harish Madhukar's vision of spirituality in arts education)

Mandakini Trivedi - Creative Head, Nateshvari Dance Gurukul.

Classical Indian Dance Programmes at the ashram.

Mandakini Trivedi training dance students at the ashram-gurukul.

Rural Programmes

Rural Programmes | The Ganapati Project

Rural Programmes | Shaniwar Shala

Spoken English sessions & Skill-building sessions.

Rural Programmes | Music For Change

BOOKS BY SWAMI SHRI HARISH MADHUKAR

Reflections of Moment

Sadhana aur Anubhuti (Hindi)

Moments in Eternity

Shashvatatil Kshana (Marathi)

Pratibimbit Kshana (Marathi)

The books are in the form of aphorisms expressing his insights into life and spirituality.

Available at:
102, Juhu Sheetal, Samarth Ramdas Marg,
Gulmohur Cross Road #9, J.V.P.D Scheme, Mumbai 400 049

~

For further information on current activities:
www.shaktiyogashrama.com

www.ingramcontent.com/pod-product-compliance
Ingram Content Group UK Ltd.
Pitfield, Milton Keynes, MK11 3LW, UK
UKHW021932200726
13853UKWH00010B/444

9 789387 242418